Moondog Verse

Moondog Verse

◆

One Independent School Teacher's Manifesto and Manual for Teaching Creative Writing to Middle Schoolers

David Winans

iUniverse, Inc.
New York Lincoln Shanghai

Moondog Verse
One Independent School Teacher's Manifesto and Manual for Teaching Creative Writing to Middle Schoolers

iUniverse, Inc.

For information address:
iUniverse, Inc.
2021 Pine Lake Road, Suite 100
Lincoln, NE 68512
www.iuniverse.com

ISBN: 0-595-33814-3

Printed in the United States of America

Contents

Acknowledgements

Though writing itself is a solitary experience, I have been blessed with the good company of hundreds of young people over the past twenty-two years, and I hope I represent them well in the following pages. Each and every one of them has enriched my life, and my deepest thanks to those who allowed me to use their poetry here. I would also like to thank Miss Betsy Tyson for her undying devotion to children and her help proofing this work. I would like to acknowledge Jack Collom and Sheryl Noethe whose wonderful book, *Poetry Everywhere*, has been a valuable resource and gave me the idea to write *Moondog Verse*. I would also like to mention Stephen Minot, a college professor of mine whose text, *Three Genres: The Writing of Poetry, Fiction and Drama*, helped me better understand the craft of writing. Thanks to colleagues past and present, Jake Dunnell, Reverend George Voight, Hugh Ogden, Richard Garten all for support and guidance over the years, and, especially, Miss Anne Gibb for her encouragement, generosity and faith in me. And, finally, thanks to my loving wife Vicki for always reminding me to follow as well as guide my students.

Greetings

We're just going to jump in here. Writing this shall be neither a chore nor ordeal. It has to come naturally or not at all. As for the title, it may at first glance appear random (one of my students' favorite words at this time). I thought about titling this book *Left to Write* which captured in part a good portion of my philosophy and had some playfulness to it, but I asked some students to choose between that and *Moondog Verse*, and, of course, the young 'uns preferred the odder of the two. Any symbolism to the chosen title? You can decide at the end of this journey. I like all three words. They sound good. I also like the word "muse" which is what all young writers need to be introduced to, their own, but how do you do that? There are different ways. Certainly it pays to keep current and adapt your lessons to what matters to the young. Change is inevitable so you must always be devising and revising writing assignments that might inspire students to write not only because they have to but because they want to. You can heed Dr. Montessori's advice and follow the child (which I believe all teachers of writing must do in part), but you also need to keep in mind the good Doctor's belief in creating the right environment. Rig the event. That's where this little offering comes into play. It's my recipe book for teachers who want to do more creative writing with their students but don't know where to or how to begin. Look, we're all in this together. If we can get young people to wake up to the discovery of their own muses, then we'll be helping keep the essential art form of poetry alive as well as producing kids with healthier minds. As important as it is to develop critical thinking skills, it is equally essential that we nudge and nurture children's imagination. I think all students should have the opportunity to take art, music and drama (or any combination of the three) daily or at least three times a week. If school systems cannot "afford" to offer such exposure to the arts, then English teachers need to step in and help fill the void. Maybe *Moondog Verse* can help you get started. Just remember: political correctness and multi-culturalism are well-intended adaptations or progressions in education, but you must teach from your passions if you wish to inspire and really connect with young people. My fifth grade makes comic books because I love to draw, and we study baseball because it was my sport as a kid (and all students need to know who Jackie Robinson was). That's where my writing lessons come from. Yours may come from a love of gardening or cooking or mountain climbing. So forget about the bureaucrats and their insidious drivel about numbers and scores and standings. Keep the passion (yours and your students') alive in the classroom, and we'll go from there.

1

Warming Up

Having taken up jogging again, I was recently reacquainted with the relevance of stretching beforehand. My calves complain not, as long as I limber up before hitting the pavement. At school, the first few weeks of every September we spend stretching with warm-up exercises. One thing we do early on is a series of *dictations* (several of which I'll speak of in depth later on). I once read an interview with the irascible Dr. Hunter S. Thompson who offered what I considered a profound recommendation for young writers. Before embarking on his own quest to write a great American novel, he sat down at the typewriter and typed word for word F. Scott Fitzgerald's *The Great Gatsby* in order to get a feel for the experience of novel writing. I thought that was such a brilliant idea. It reminded me of how Bob Dylan learned and copied Woody Guthrie's songs and style of performing them before creating his own body of work. Dictation has a number of benefits. It requires students to be good listeners (and we know that writers must be good listeners, language being as much sound as symbol). Dictation of poetry in particular exposes students to typography (the spacing and arrangement of words and lines of words). It also gives them that experience of getting a feel for the piece of writing.

Another worthwhile warm-up exercise is **writing with your other hand**. I always tell the students a personal story about a lady named Jane Cable with whom I once taught when I was just out of college. She had been on the review board of teachers and students who interviewed me for my first teaching job. I remembered that she spoke in a kind voice which helped me relax in a rather imposing situation. I also noted that she wore a sweater draped over her shoulders and constantly wrote notes with her left hand. A month later, having been hired, I was at the school meeting my new colleagues and I walked into the science room to thank this lady for her calming presence during my interview. It was then that I noticed beneath the ever-present draped sweater that she had no right arm. It was the only thing the cancer had claimed, and she didn't let it slow her down one bit. I also got a good view of her handwriting which was beautiful. She told me that yes, she was originally right-handed, but now she was a lefty. Though I knew her for such a short period of time, Jane has always been one of my inspirations. To this day I ask my students to spend time writing with their other hand. I explain that with effort and practice they could all learn to write neatly with their other hand. Anything is possible once you put your mind to it and determine to succeed. A simple platitude no doubt, but a worthy one nonetheless.

Over the years, my students have always loved getting me off track to discuss something they want to talk about which is not necessarily part of the curriculum. They think they're pulling a fast one on me, but really, that's where some of the magic happens, so it's fine with me. Thus, in this little tome I'll have some *deviations*. The first of these regards the escape clause. Isn't that something especially American, the escape clause? I like the idea of wiggle room and of allowing myself to be impulsive. I think the creative mind works best on impulse. W.B. Yeats and other master craftsmen may disagree, but I love spontaneous moments in art, that rush of inspiration that remains unvarnished. Young people are impulsive by nature, and some brilliant creative writing can come out of that. Encouraging students to be themselves, to follow their instincts, to risk embarrassment, these may not be part of any standard manual, but that's where you must begin if you truly wish to nurture a love of and desire to write creatively.

I'm going to deviate some more. Remember when the character of "Benjamin" in *The Graduate* was given the advice that "the future is in plastics"? I have only one word to say…**nature**. The future is in nature, and young people desperately need to be introduced to and indoctrinated in the natural world. The Romantic poets of the 1800's pointed this out, as do our great poets of modern times such as Seamus Heaney. Suburbia and its various electronic elixirs strip ordinary children of their imagination (though the innately creative ones are somehow able to unearth profundity in even the most mundane existence). Getting young people to take nature walks, grow gardens, and appreciate the "outdoors" cannot be emphasized enough. Early in autumn, I take students with their journals around the campus collecting nouns. We go to the Lower School playground to reminisce about our Montessori and Kindergarten years. We go to the beach (which happens to be across the street) to write poetry and observations. Getting young people to identify the writing experience beyond sitting at a desk in a room with four walls is important if you seek to instill a desire to write. My main goal is to get kids to want to write. Once that happens, students are far more receptive to learning the craft of writing.

Two other warm-up exercises emphasize the importance of detail. Students generally arrive in my class aware of adjectives and adverbs as words used for description. I attempt to impress upon them how nouns and verbs are equally important for good description. I'll take a strong verb over a slew of mediocre adjectives any day. **The Hands** exercise is simple and effective. Students trace their hands on a piece of paper. Then, within the hands or around the hands or outside of the hands, they write a dozen uses for those hands using strong, descriptive verbs such as "yanking" weeds from the soil, "gripping" the lacrosse stick, "untangling" fishing line. Inevitably, one or more adventurous youngsters will write about whacking a sibling or picking up dog poop. It is up to the teacher's discretion how to handle such situations, but I tend to allow them a fair amount of freedom of expression (as long as they use strong verbs, but no expletives). Concerning *swear words,* and considering we live in a time when pop culture is oversaturated with their use, I think it might behoove English teachers to research the origins of such terms and be equipped for honest, thoughtful discussion of their allure, stigma, benefits, and consequences of their use. Perhaps it's too fine a line to walk, but knowledge not only empowers the individual, but can lead to transformation. A fuller understanding of such terms' origins and why they are considered offensive may influence some young people to pause before using such language. Ah, a brief deviation. Now on to **The Room** exercise.

The Room exercise is also quite simple, but not necessarily easy to pull off. Students are asked to write a description of one of their rooms at home. The catch is that they can only use nouns and verbs; no adjectives or adverbs allowed. It is a challenge and one way to strengthen one's appreciation and use of nouns and verbs as descriptive words. It also introduces to students the idea of writing without clutter. Examples are always handy for such exercises, so I wrote one about our classroom.

Classroom

It is walls, ceiling, floor. There are windows which are rectangles. The carpet is fiber. There are spots where water fell. The roof leaks. There is a hole in the wall where a teacher threw a chair. The shelves have books. Books are stories, information, knowledge for students who occupy chairs made of wood. The desks have scratches, names carved in them. On the windowsill rests a saxophone, photographs in frames, cards, memorabilia. There are bags used for carrying books, computer, stereo, television, poetry, boxes, dictionaries. Students wear khakis, shirts and shoes. The desk of teacher includes mugs, scissors, screwdriver, stapler, basket, paper and pens. Stains from water appear on ceiling made of squares of cork. There are vents, a thermostat, blackboard, maps, artwork. The eyes of students watch me. The hands of students hold pens put to paper. They think, concentrate, formulate and write words that express ideas and thoughts. Trees, sky, colors, noise exist beyond the walls of classroom. Inside the room, desks creak, students shuffle papers, legs rub, breathing continues, noses sniff. Students stretch limits of thought and chase imagination into realms of discovery. Enlightenment happens. Life is a path that goes beyond walls and classrooms. Knowledge awaits. Experience informs. The walls remain.

The **Room** exercise can be used to reinforce parts of speech lessons, sharpen observation skills, and introduce *personification.*

One more warm-up exercise that never fails to excite young people is the **Mind Trip**. This is a word association game that a freelance songwriter/English teacher showed me back in the early 80's at the New Independent High School in New London, Connecticut. I cannot for the life of me remember his name, but I'll never forget what he showed me. The **Mind Trip** acquaints students with the idea of association. The class begins with a word and a student is asked to quickly think of the first word that comes to mind when he or she sees that word. Then the next student is asked to respond in similar fashion to the first student's word. You go around the room until everyone has contributed a word. Next you try to string phrases together out of the word list. You may add words and even skip over a few of the words on the list. Sometimes you create total nonsense (which students enjoy), and other times you actually come up with the beginning of a poem. Next you break the class up into groups of four or five and have them create a **mind trip** list and hopefully after that a **poem**. There can be as many steps as you wish to have. If you are interested in having the students work on creating a polished, finished product, you can suggest they spend more time eliminating and adding words from the original list or carefully pruning and shaping the phrases strung together from the list. In such a case you have students involved in *revision*, an aspect of writing which will be emphasized more and more as they progress through the system.

Word List	**Mind Trip Poem**
Ocean	The ocean waves
Waves	call all surfers
Surf	racing with waxed boards
Board	baking under
Wax	the fiery sun
Candle	until water cools
Fire	them
Sun	waves crashing
Water	the great mysteries
Ocean	go unsolved
Waves	today we live
Crash	life
Plane	we surf
Bermuda Triangle	
Mystery	
Death	
Life	

These are just a few warm-up or "stretching" exercises to help limber up the mind and make students less timid or uncertain about the prospect of being asked to be a creative writer. The idea is to get students to that point where they want to express themselves not because they have to, but because it matters to them. Many of you teachers out there working in this noblest of professions undoubtedly have your own methods and exercises for getting students started. Those of you who do likely share my view that pre-writing is a crucial part of the process, especially for the many of us who do not take to writing naturally. You must begin somewhere and so September (or nowadays the last two weeks of August) is a good time to get ready for the season ahead.

2

"Digging" and Other Exercises

Always start your students off with a good example or blueprint of what you want them to attempt. That means you have to read and search for good pieces of writing. I have been very fortunate to know lovely parents such as Eleanor Rauch who turned me on to Seamus Heaney. As fate would have it, I later happened to have the good fortune of hearing him read his work in Sligo, Ireland. Eleanor had introduced me to him by way of a book called *Seeing Things.* When I came across "Digging," I couldn't help but notice the use of *simile, metaphor, assonance, alliteration* and a wonderful use of vivid *imagery.* It is plainspoken, yet profound. His choice of verbs is meticulous, his ability to create a sense of rootedness and the passage of time, affinity for (yet independence from) family and tradition, and his description of the pen as both gun and spade could lead to much discussion in a high school lit class. I use the poem with Seventh Graders because it has concrete imagery and is a good example of *metaphor.* It also allows us to discuss personal experience as a primary source for creative writing. We are always "digging" to understand ourselves and our experiences. As much as we write to express our ideas and feelings, we also write to learn about ourselves and better understand our world and our place in it. Writing is a quest. John Keats spoke of this; Seamus Heaney carries on the message.

Digging

Between my finger and my thumb
The squat pen rests; snug as a gun.

Under my window, a clean rasping sound
When the spade sinks into gravelly ground:
My father, digging. I look down

Till his straining rump among the flowerbeds
Bends low, comes up twenty years away
Stooping in rhythm through potato drills
Where he was digging.

The coarse boot nestled on the lug, the shaft
Against the inside knee was levered firmly.
He rooted out tall tops, buried the bright edge deep
To scatter new potatoes that we picked
Loving their cool hardness in our hands.

By God, the old man could handle a spade.
Just like his old man.

My grandfather cut more turf in a day
Than any other man on Toner's bog.
Once I carried him milk in a bottle
Corked sloppily with paper. He straightened up
To drink it, then fell to right away
Nicking and slicing neatly, heaving sods
Over his shoulder, going down and down
For the good turf. Digging.

The cold smell of potato mould, the squelch and slap
Of soggy peat, the curt cuts of an edge
Through living roots awaken in my head.
But I've no spade to follow men like them.

Between my finger and my thumb
The squat pen rests.
I'll dig with it.

Students must read this poem aloud. It will help them spot the *assonance* and *alliteration* Heaney uses. Afterwards, you might discuss the different settings, what the poem tells us about the family's history, the use of strong descriptive verbs, and what the poet might then dig for. Bring in a shovel and have the students attempt to recreate the movement of the father digging in the potato field to better understand how specific Heaney's use of imagery. You could discuss the *symbolism* of the potato in Irish culture and what peat is used for. Then ask your students to write their own "Digging" poem in which they use some form of *metaphor* and connect several different scenes from one or more generations of their family. That sounds like a lot to ask of them, but it is the challenging assignments that generate the most interesting results. You can ask them what their interests are and if they can somehow relate one of those interests to activities, hobbies or jobs of their parents or grandparents. You are now imploring your students to examine their relationship to their families as well as directing them towards a fertile source of material for writing assignments. A youngster who enjoys flying kites might relate that to a time he went sailing with his granddad or a student who gets bored easily in school might learn that it was much the same for his dad or mom when they were his age. What a wonderful discovery to be part of a family tradition. As old family friend Dr. Lombardo once said to Chet Buffum in reference to his son's similar habits, "Chester, you plant potatoes, you get potatoes."

Oh, by the way, insist that the students not rhyme this piece. You say the word "poetry" and many students immediately assume you must rhyme. Tell them this is not the case anymore. If there are youngsters who want to rhyme, design a separate assignment for writing in rhyme. For "Digging" have them concentrate on using vivid verbs and strong imagery such as "the spade sinks into gravelly ground" or "the milk in a bottle corked sloppily with paper." Suggest that they try using *assonance* and *alliteration* if not overwhelmed by the other requirements of the assignment. It never hurts to give them options and possibilities as added incentives as long as you allow for different learning styles and how some students will want very clearly spelled out instructions.

Family Ties: The Relative Time Exercise

I've often heard it said that kids today are too present-minded. Implied in this observation is that they lack curiosity about and appreciation for the past or history. Doesn't every generation say that about its children? I myself think it's a false accusation. Young people are often intrigued by different periods of time, especially those glamorized by television or the movies. I remember how as a teenager I became fascinated with and even longed for the 1950's after I saw the movie *American Graffiti*. It was smack dab in the middle of the gaudy 1970's, and I suddenly longed for straight-legged pants and the music of Chuck Berry, Fats Domino and the Coasters. At boarding school I would listen to Wolfman Jack's radio show while next door the monotonous thud of Led Zeppelin and various other heavy metal or hard rock bands reminded me how out of place I felt in that decade. It was also at this time that I began to become more interested in American history which leads me to suspect that we develop an interest in a subject such as history later in adolescence. Still, it is never too early to encourage younger students to gain a better sense of where they come from. Most English teachers I know teach historical context when discussing a novel. Students should also have the opportunity to learn about their own family history. The **Relative Time** writing exercise is technically more an expository writing assignment, yet I include it here because it fits in with my recurring message that personal experience is such a fertile primary source for young writers. You as the teacher can establish your own format requirements. The students can write the piece as a five-paragraph essay with specific paragraphs designated for introduction, local setting (time and place), more general setting (what was happening in the world of politics and culture at the time), the subject's experiences and observations, and the writer's thoughts and impressions. Other options are to have the students write a **You Were There** style piece or present it as an interview such as you might find in a magazine. The pre-writing work, however, should be clearly spelled out as the crucial part of this assignment. Each person must choose someone they can personally interview. The student must then decide what period of that person's life to concentrate on, and do some research so that they are familiar with the specific period of time before writing a dozen or so questions for the interview. Another valuable writing experience is to have the students transpose the interview and present an accurate transcript. It is essentially "grunt" work, but it also exposes the student to how people speak with inflections and pauses for thought and any personal traits that distinguish us as individuals. Students are also learning about *documentation*, *primary sources*, and other people's *perspectives*. It is also a positive way to involve family members and help keep the family history alive.

Personal writing comes in many forms and can be encouraged and developed in school in a variety of assignments. Having students keep a **daily journal** over an extended period of time has its merits despite their often initial resistance. You as the teacher can come up with some offbeat or clever observation assignments for the journal writing such as writing down lunchroom conversations or comments overheard from adults or routines at home or in school. Ask the students to write **stream of consciousness pieces** for a week or two. It has been my experience that young people enjoy writing which asks them to free associate, i.e. the popularity of the **Mind Trip** game. Another form of personal writing is the friendly letter which sounds dull and generic, but again you can put a twist on the assignment by asking your charges to write a letter to their favorite cartoon or television character or celebrity. Suggest that it can be someone the student likes or dislikes. The letter can become a tribute or a critique. Ask your students to express how they feel and then elaborate. It is important that they become aware of and learn the several formats for letter writing be it business letter or thank you note or letter to a friend. Then simply encourage them always to write as if what they have to say matters.

It is inherently true that **personal experience writing** gets deeper and more complex in later years of adolescence. Youngsters between the ages of ten and thirteen should not be forced to "get deep" or deal with difficult emotions in their writing. Many children simply do not have much experience with sorrow or fear or anger. However, some young people have had traumatic experiences early on in life, and everyone has the above-mentioned emotions in various degrees on a daily basis. Getting young students to feel comfortable enough to write about such feelings (whether it be doing poorly on a math test or the passing of a relative or being hurt by a friend) is one of those tricks of the trade I do not necessarily know how to produce. It simply happens that sometimes young people feel comfortable enough with me (or themselves) to write about things that bother them or have left a strong impression on them. I save many of my former students' pieces, and there is one in particular that cuts so deep and always gets a sympathetic, sometimes empathetic response from current students when I read it to them.

How Come?

How come people tell
    secrets and leave
        me out?
How come when I ask someone
    to play a game and they say,
    "No," they play a game
        with someone else
        right after I ask them?
I guess nobody likes
        me.
How come nobody invites me
to sleep over?

Kids can be cruel. Sometimes they have great role models. This little poem made me feel so sad. The use of the word "no" and how the others shun and isolate the author simply but effectively captures what this young girl was experiencing. To me this is profound poetry. You cannot help but be moved by it. Not every student is in a position to write this type of heartfelt piece. However, everyone can write about themselves and how they feel about something in particular. Three exercises that have worked well for me are the **I Remember Assignment,** the **Value of Friendship Narrative Composition,** and one I gave our seniors, Eighth graders in this case, called **Looking Back Before Moving On**.

I Remember

When possible I like to use student work as examples. It promotes their work and suggests to other students that what they have to say is valid and important. Students are often impressed and inspired by listening to the work of writers their age. For **I Remember,** I currently use a piece by a former student of mine named Margot who had a knack for using rich detail and specific memories. This is a fine example of vivid writing. It creates pictures in the reader's mind and also reflects the personality of its author.

I remember the first time I heard 'Brown-eyed Girl.' I had a tummy ache. My dad played it on his saxophone to make me feel better.
I remember the first time I saw water slide off a duck's back. I was swimming with my duckies in the baby pool in my backyard.
I remember meeting Carolina, my new babysitter. I loved her so much. She taught me how to speak Spanish and told me bugs aren't icky, they're fun.
I remember my dream to be a mermaid so I could learn how to dance and sing under the water.
I remember the first time I picked up a lacrosse stick. I was four. My dad and brother were playing and I wanted to play, too. My dad threw the ball to me. I missed it and the ball hit me in the head. I learned to wear a helmet when playing with the big boys.
I remember seeing on television people cooking eggs on the road. When I tried cooking eggs, I failed. It must have been because it was during the winter.
I remember the first time I saw my brother surf. It always looked like fun to me. However, I always thought it would hurt if you fell off.
I remember my grandma Betts always telling stories, always talking about something.
I remember my grandpa telling her to be quiet because she was hurting his ears.
I remember writing all over Mommy's important papers.

I remember my father showing me pictures of where he used to live in Nepal. I thought he was weird because he had really long hair and didn't shave. He looked funny to me.

I remember the first time I saw my little sister. She was so small. I loved her, except when she started crying. I asked the nurse, 'Can we get a new baby that doesn't cry so much?'

I remember when my mother told me everyone is short when they are young, but that I will grow into a beautiful flower. I sat outside in the garden waiting to grow.

I remember my old school had Crazy Hat Day. I was the only one who made his or her hat. I thought my hat was the coolest.

I remember the look on my mom and dad's faces the first time I called them Lisa and Michael. They told me not to call them that. I started calling them Mrs. Tiernan and Mr. Tiernan. They were stunned.

I remember my father telling me for the very first time that the University of North Carolina at Chapel Hill was the best place on Earth. We were watching a football game. UNC was up by a lot of points. There were tons of Dad's friends there. I was wearing my UNC cheerleading outfit with my blue and white pom-poms. I had a weird looking foot painted on my right cheek. I had an itch there but I wasn't allowed to scratch it or the little foot would smear.

I remember the day I told my mom and dad I was a big girl. They didn't come up to say goodnight. I stomped all the way down the stairs and to their room where I put my hands on my hips and yelled, "Aren't you coming up to say goodnight?" They replied, "We thought you were a big girl." I told them, "Yes, I am, but it is okay to have your mommy and daddy tuck you in bed." They laughed, but they came upstairs, said goodnight, kissed me and turned off the lights.

I remember that night I slept better than I ever have because I got my parents to do what I wanted them to do. I thought that I could control them for a long, long time. I was finally a big girl, I thought.

The assignment calls for the student to think back on his or her "life so far." I ask them to think of twenty or so moments that stick out in their memory of personal experience. They may be memories of time spent at camp, school or with the family on vacation. Students might write about "first times" or discoveries. They may write out memories in chronological order or in a more free form fashion. I ask them to zero in on specifics ("I remember the first time I saw water slide off a duck's back"). Students may include how they felt at the time, what the world looked like at the time to them, and the key part of the memory that makes it something to remember.

The Value of Friendship (A Narrative Composition)

"I've never had friends like the ones I had when I was twelve. Jesus, does anybody?" was the closing quote by the narrator in the coming of age movie *Stand By Me* based on a novella by Stephen King. One of the main themes to emerge from this story was the essential value of friendship. A similar theme is explored in the movie *Now And Then*. Both films focus on a wide range of experiences and emotions that the youngsters share and cope with as they grapple with growing up. There is comedy and sorrow, adventure and reflection, light and darkness in these stories, and both are told through a **specific point of view**. Being that in each of these movies one character looks back and tells the story, they are good examples of **first-person narrative**.

One particular year after a group of my eighth graders watched these two films, I asked them to assume the voice of a character (hopefully their own) to tell a story that involved the student and a friend or a group of friends. They were asked to describe those friends and their particular experiences with them. I then challenged the student as writer to capture the **value of that friendship** in the story or composition. The piece may be about a particular incident or period of time (one summer at camp, a memorable vacation, a fishing trip). I tried to impress upon them that what they chose to include (references to music, clothes, news events, expressions) would reflect the time period being described. Meanwhile, the commentary itself (what they have to say about these characters, i.e. friends) would indicate what those friends mean to the writer. In other words, be conscious of what you are trying to say. Choose your words carefully. Say what you mean and mean what you say. To a large extent creative writing is about self-awareness. Students need to know and understand this point.

Looking Back Before Moving On

For our seniors I often finish the year with an assignment similar to **I Remember**. I talk to them about impending graduation and the end of a chapter in their lives. Some students attend our school for eleven years of their young lives. I point out that they have undoubtedly experienced a wide range of "moments," both personal and public. Thus, they have impressions, memories, and surely some life lessons. I give the students four weeks for this assignment. I ask them to begin by jotting down in their journals memories, recollections, what happened at the time and how they felt about it, ways they might have done things differently, things that over the years have annoyed them, humorous episodes, experiences that humbled or taught them something about themselves or others. I ask them to talk to friends and classmates to see if they recall situations differently or concur. Next, the student must piece together a rough draft. Then I instruct them to put the rough draft away for several days. Afterwards, come back and read it with fresh eyes. This may help them revise the draft: add, subtract, change wording. I suggest that the final work may include drawings or a photograph or any personal touch they may choose to add. The piece may contain one important memory or a series of memories. I also suggest that they write with an attitude or particular point of view (again emphasizing *narrative voice*). Perhaps a specific theme will emerge. I also note that if they choose to write about several or many memories, perhaps they could consider unifying them. The recollections might paint a certain picture or could be seen as pieces to a puzzle. I conclude with the advice, "Write from your strengths."

Baseball, Jazz and the Constitution

The poet Gerald Early has suggested that when people centuries from now look back at this civilization of these United States, we will be remembered for three perfect designs: baseball, jazz music, and the Constitution. What a fabulous notion. Some time-tested advice for young teachers is to teach from your strengths, and what you are passionate about makes up one of those strengths. I happen to love music, American history, and baseball, so despite my political views I'd probably get along quite well with the columnist George Will. He and others help narrate Ken Burns' nine-part documentary on the game of baseball, sections of which I use in my unit on the national pastime. Baseball has so many fascinating elements to it (even its greatest stars fail seven out of ten times to get a hit), contradictions, wonderful examples of irony, built-in myths, its own colorful language, and at its heart one of our nations' greatest triumphs in the Jackie Robinson story. So I use a month-long lesson on the history of baseball to teach students about race relations, free marketplace, the necessity of teamwork, how things in life originate and evolve, the importance of perseverance and being aware of past injustices. Of course, we also cover superstition and the idea of eternal hope when we spend the last four days learning about the dreaded Curse of the Bambino and its effect on the Boston Red Sox.

My mentor for more than twenty years, Miss Anne Gibb taught me several essential teaching tips, including that memory work is valuable, good for stretching and strengthening the young mind. In the baseball unit, I ask students to memorize "The Star-Spangled Banner," "Take Me Out to the Ballgame," a slew of timeless quotes, and between thirty and fifty baseball terms. We have a baseball vocabulary test and general information and history highlights test. Students also must write either a creative writing piece or expository composition on the life and times of Jackie Robinson. Then we go outside and learn "pickle" or "rundown" and cap it off with a softball game. For some odd reason my esteem amongst the boys in my class increases greatly during this month, yet I must point out that more often than not, the top test scores have as many girls' names on them as boys'.

The centerpiece of the baseball unit each year is the Jackie Robinson story which opens the door to any number of topics for discussion and study. Jackie Robinson was referred to as a "race man" or one who seeks to improve the conditions not only for himself but, in this case, other African-Americans. He is a heroic figure in every sense of the word, a man who endured taunts and jeers, opposing players spiking him, pitchers throwing at his head, angry anonymous letters that threatened to harm his family. His story is one of suffering the ugliness of racism and the neo-slavery of segregation. And yet he never comes off as a victim because he keeps his infamous temper under control when it counts and ultimately prevails in helping pave the way for other black athletes to join the major leagues and help finally integrate baseball. Mr. Robinson's story is also about keeping one's promise or being true to one's word. His deal with Brooklyn Dodgers owner Branch Rickey was to not fight back for three years, and it is clearly evident that Mr. Rickey chose Mr. Robinson as much for the content of his character as his playing ability. Mr. Rickey, meanwhile, determines to integrate baseball in large part because of a commitment he made to himself as a young manager of a college team when he witnessed a black ballplayer, who had been denied a room at a whites only hotel, sitting in Mr. Rickey's room pulling at the skin of his arms and muttering, "If I could just take this off I'd be like everybody else." Both men determine to bring about a long overdue change in American society and to learn their story is as important as any other event in American history for the topics of fairness, equality, and "liberty and justice for all" lie at the core of our country's tragic failings and potential for greatness.

I have two writing assignments I alternate between using, but both provide a word bank or information key. Students must choose a minimum of fifteen of the following words and terms: Ebbets Field, race man, rookie of the year (Robinson was the first such designated award winner), base stealer, run producer, Negro Leagues, post-World War II, Big Show, spikes, curses, epithets, racial slurs, racism, prejudice, segregation, "tons of guts" (Ted Williams quote), danc-ing off the base, "All eyes riveted", self-control, pride, a higher goal, grandson of a slave, April 15, 1947. I also include the names of key characters including Branch Rickey, Pee Wee Reese, who was a white southerner and one of the first Dodger players to accept and stand up for Mr. Robinson, and the new commissioner of baseball, Happy Chandler, who proclaimed, "If a man can catch bullets for his country, he ought to be allowed to catch a baseball." I also make a list of words from our vocabulary workbook which includes transform, obstacle, challenge, grim, loathe, rouse, harsh, heroic, oppose, accelerate, confident, exult, boisterous, illuminate, tolerant, and change. I offer quotes such as broadcaster Red Barber's "I learned from Jackie Robinson to be a better person" and Mr. Rickey's question to Mr. Robinson, "Do you have the guts to not fight back?"

From here the students either write a non-rhyming narrative poem in which they tell the story in a series of stanzas, or are given a five paragraph format in which I specify what information goes where. For instance, the first paragraph would establish time and place. The story takes place in America after World War II when there was still segregation, including in baseball with the Negro leagues. This was a period of time when the owners of major league baseball teams refused to allow black ballplayers to play in the all-white league. It was also a period of time when the United States had helped liberate millions of Jewish people and much of Europe from the clutches of Nazi Germany. In the next paragraph students are asked to introduce and describe Branch Rickey and explain why he wanted to integrate baseball. They should also mention Commis-sioner Chandler being open to the idea, unlike the previous commissioner, Judge Kenesaw Mountain Landis, who refused to consider the possibility. Paragraph three is dedicated to describing Jackie Robinson, his background as a child raised by his hardworking mother, his teen years as a star college athlete, his tenure in the army, and his time as a player in the Negro League. Paragraph four requires a description of Mr. Robinson's meeting with and promise to Mr. Rickey and the resulting first year in which he endured hardships and prevailed victoriously. The final paragraph asks for a summation of why Mr. Robinson is heroic and why what he did was important for his country as well as for the game of baseball.

This is clearly an assignment where I'm leading the horse to water, but I occa-sionally feel the need to do so. It is a great opportunity to discuss paragraph building, the use of a topic sentence, using detail to support a statement. Perhaps it is too much fill in the blanks and therefore not really a creative writing assignment, but it requires the students to use detail and specific language which is always a valuable lesson for writers.

Jazz Writing-The Conversational Style Piece

"Kidspeak" is precious, funny, and a part of one's identity. Adults sound stupid, even pathetic, if they try to appropriate it without a genuine tongue in cheek approach acknowledging that this is yours, not mine, I'm aware of and having fun with you, but not as a put down, if you know what I mean. Grown ups, trying to sound hip only makes you more square (squarer for you purists out there). But understand that young people have their own language and should be encouraged to use it in their writing.

You might begin this assignment with some **Journal** work. Ask the students to write down pieces of conversation they hear at lunch, in the hallways, at dinnertime, in the locker room. Remind them that a writer's ears are as valuable as his eyes. Good writers are good listeners. Listen for what is said and how it is said. Be alert and attentive to phrasing and enunciation. Students must learn to focus and exercises such as these encourage that. Write down several dozen quotes or passages of conversation. Try this exercise a couple times during the day or over a few days. Gather and collect before you select. These are your "riffs" you can come back to and use at your discretion. Note also that this is only one part of **Jazz Writing**, more a warm-up than anything else.

Now ask the students to choose a topic that comes directly from daily experience: the kick ball game at recess, eating lunch with friends, the morning drive to school. Explain that they are to write their piece as if they were having a conversation with a friend in "kidspeak" and that random thoughts or observations are okay, impressions of people, inside jokes, made-up expressions are acceptable and encouraged, and then tell them that a theme or point to the piece must emerge by the end.

I like and use the term **Jazz Writing** not because I'm such a huge fan of jazz music, but the term itself conjures up what I think young writers should be exposed to. "Jazz" implies or connotes improvisation and individual interpretation while "jazzy" suggests unrestraint or animation. I suppose you could substitute the term "rap", but upon hearing that word the tendency for young people is to once again think of rhyming couplets which inevitably for many leads to forced rhymes which defeats the whole purpose of writing. Writing in the initial stage should be unrestrained and animated which young people know a thing or two about. One's personality should be encouraged to emerge on the page. The term "jazz" also suggests the idea of "riffing" which in writing appears as a series of associated ideas (something comedians do all the time in their stage acts, Robin Williams perhaps the master of them all). Kids riff off of one another all the time in those moments outside of the classroom and that's where great material lies in wait for the young writer. And remember that kids have "big ears" and those ears can be trained to listen to language and how it is used, so asking them to write about a conversation is directing them to one of the sources of writing.

A Students' Bill of Rights

For many young people democracy is a much ballyhooed concept that may exist in the adult world but is seldom experienced in "kid-dom." This is often brought to my attention by my students who ultimately convince me that they need to exercise their right to vote to get the practice for later in life. So sometimes we determine writing assignments or deadlines or what book we are going to read next by majority rule. I also throw in my two cents about how with freedom comes responsibility and when given the opportunity to make a choice, one must make the most of it and choose wisely. "Sure, Mr. Winans, whatever you say, but can we vote now?"

The **Bill of Rights** writing exercise, however, did not evolve out of such classroom discussions but instead was a proposal by several students one day when we were trying to settle an argument about the daily kickball game at recess which led into a chaotic clambering about fairness in general. The class's elected officers sat down and produced a list of fifth grader rights and rules of the games played at recess as well as a preamble patterned after the *Bill of Rights* in the *Constitution*. Voila! Another engaging writing activity is born of student interest. Students will write as if it matters if given the opportunity to write about what matters to them. The study of history can seem uninteresting to young people living in their insular world of immediacy, but if you can tap into that world of the here and now and then apply or adapt the history to the moment, then learning happens quite naturally. This brings me to an essential truth pointed out by John Ashberry: "I didn't really get a feeling for the poetry of the past until I had discovered modern poetry. Then I began to see how nineteenth-century poetry wasn't just something lifeless in an ancient museum but must have grown out of the lives of the people who wrote it." This reconnects us to the idea of understanding the context out of which something was written. If you can get students to write from personal experience in any way or form, you are impressing upon them this lesson regarding context as well as showing them that writing is a vital means of expression and communication. The students' **Bill of Rights** did not solve all of the problems involving peer interaction that year, but I never heard anymore about unfairness regarding the kickball games which was a step in the right direction.

You Were There

This is an oldie but goodie. When I started teaching at my current school twenty-two years ago, I taught American history as well as English to my fifth graders. I knew that somehow I had to make history more interesting to eleven-year-olds, so I devised several projects such as debates, play acting, and the **You Were There** research and writing a story assignment. I remembered reading that series of books such as *You Were There on the Oregon Trail* when I was in elementary school, and I liked the idea of a research project where students could also use their imagination. I asked them to read up on their subject and get the historical facts accurate but be creative about what the characters might have said and thought and felt. I also asked the students to concentrate on one particular event and avoid telling the historical figure's life story or the event's facts only. I wanted them to make it a story (to bring out the *story* in his*tory*) and think about what it might have been like to live through and witness that place and time. Nowadays we have so many documentaries and videos that conveniently do this for us which in a way rob students of the creative experience, so my advice is to consider this type of activity instead of plopping in a videotape.

Being given the opportunity to pretend or make believe should not be underestimated. One period of my own childhood was filled with afternoons of romping around my grandmother's woods with my buddy, Fred Buffum. We were Daniel Boone and Davy Crockett in our coonskin caps carrying fairly authentic-looking flintlock rifles. Most of my adult friends speak fondly of similar experiences growing up. Today's children, however, are often whisked from one supervised, organized activity to the next and miss out on valuable time of play and imagination. We should not deny our children these precious moments. The poet Wordsworth once lamented, "The world is too much with us," and we must pay heed to this truth and seek ways to provide children some less structured, free time to be children.

Structuring a Poem: The "Ianing" Exercise

There is a patched up but still slightly visible hole in my classroom wall that students traditionally ask me about at the beginning of each school year. From the mouths of older students, my young fifth graders are fed the story about how that hole got there. Legend has it that I threw a kid headfirst into the wall; a very small kid for the hole is less than two inches wide. Of course there is a general consensus amongst even the most impressionable that this is just a made-up or hugely exaggerated story but nonetheless a good distraction from the regularly scheduled lesson. The actual truth of the matter that I maintain to this day is that a rather rambunctious group of fives were refusing to settle down one day so I, as I occasionally did in those days, took my chair and banged it on the floor to quiet down the rowdy ones and restore order. But this time the chair flew out of my hands and planted itself in my wall. Yes, I was not displaying enough self-control that day, and in all honesty I may have in the heat of the moment directed the chair sideways as opposed to downward. But it surely quieted down the rabble rousers and gave me an edge for awhile. Of course nowadays I'd be sent to anger management classes. At any rate the ringleader of the boys who instigated such inappropriate behavior on my part was a tousle-haired youth named Ian who was quick-witted and sharp-tongued and a delight.

When it came to writing, Ian cared not for rules and instruction, but he wrote with a wonderful sense of humor and often used vivid imagery. Once, however, I asked the class to recount a personal experience, but instead of writing a composition I instructed them to write in a more poetic format using four to five short stanzas. Most of the class dutifully did as I asked, but Ian, of course, handed in a paragraph; a paragraph, mind you, that he was quite proud of. Now Ian quite possibly was being defiant, but in this case I realized two things. One was that Ian had likely never been asked to write stanzas and was not confident enough to attempt doing so at the time. He also had written a solid little narrative rich in material to use in a short four-stanza piece. So I showed Ian how to take his paragraph and transform it.

"I was going fishing with Bobby. He was using a rapola. The day before he caught five fish in the same spot! It was in the middle of the day. We were crossing the road when my brother Carson Hunt ran out in the road and started to call Bobby "a nerd, a geek, and an idiot." Bob turned quickly and the fish hook went into my leg! I went

to the hospital and waited for an hour. The doctor finally came in and took the fish hook out. After I left the hospital, I went to football practice."

Kids are impulsive, impatient and indestructible. Ian captured all of this in his short narrative. Now I sat down with him and took the paragraph apart and pieced it back together as a William Carlos Williams-style poem:

Fishing with Bobby
He and his rapola
Caught five the day before
In this same spot!

Middle of the day
We crossed the road
When Carson Hunt called
Bobby a geek.

Next thing I know
His fish hook's
In my leg
And I spend an hour
In the hospital.

Doctor finally unhooks me
Just in time for
Football practice.

Maybe Ian appreciated the idea of the doctor "unhooking" him and throwing him back into the world to go to football practice. I tried to point out to him that in this format you can bring out the main points in a succinct way and say more with less. Some students genuinely rejoice in the idea of saying more with less, though that is something one must work on developing a knack for. This lesson returns us to the idea of writing being a "craft." As much as I try to teach writing as an art form, it is equal parts craft; the two go hand in hand. I understand Robert Lowell when he declares, "Writing isn't a craft, that is, something for which you learn the skills and go on turning out. It must come from some deep impulse, deep inspiration. That can't be taught, it can't be what you use in teaching." In this sense, the best a teacher can do is once again booby-trap the room and provide opportunities for young writers to come upon their own inspiration. But even our youngest writers must be encouraged to learn and apply format and structures such as couplets and stanzas and the use of meter. Even the great jazz musicians known for their spontaneity and improvisational skills know the scales and how to arrange notes and produce melodies. I understand and agree with Lowell but also find room for Archibald MacLeish's dictum: "The first discipline is the realization that there is a discipline—that all art begins and ends with discipline, that any art is first and foremost a craft."

Catching Fire

Some years back I had a student who would hit the beach with her dad and catch some waves before going to school. What a great way to start the day. She was part of a large class that included a pack of boys who loved surfing and music and likely only tolerated school because at least they were with their friends. Four of the boys put together a garage band they dubbed the Surfing Eyeballs. They even held a concert at the end of lunch once in our outside eating area, the Pavilion. I always like to encourage and support young people learning and playing any form of musical instrument. How many of us as adults wish that our parents had insisted we stick with those piano or guitar lessons? Learning to read and play music is an excellent discipline and gives a lifetime of pleasure. It puts one in touch with the movement of sound. Writing also involves rhythm and manipulating sound, so having an understanding and appreciation of music benefits the young writer. Students need to be encouraged to write with an awareness that what they write will be read aloud. The sound of words matters.

Now the surfing, guitar-playing boys in this class were not great grammarians, but they were game for trying their hand at creative writing exercises, especially when given plenty of latitude concerning subject matter. Several of the boys, when not writing about violent battles between hideous beasts, would pen pieces about surfing. From this I came up with the idea of a writing assignment which required students to use as many words as they could from a **"surfing lingo dictionary"** that accompanied the box set of surfing hits entitled *Cowabunga*. The domain-specific language includes some terrific verbs (amped, eat it, shredding), a wide assortment of adjectives (including kid-friendly words such as hairy, bogus, stoked and mondo) as well as nouns that sound funny (hodad, honkers, grommet). This exercise introduces young people to words as sound images, the flexibility of language and how people, especially the young, regularly adapt language to their own activities.

This is a recurring theme in my English classes. Each subject we learn, each extracurricular activity or hobby, each line of work we enter into, all have their own lexicon of words, terms, phrases. And this is the material writers use to mold and shape their works. When we study baseball we come across Stengelese, Yogiisms (including such profundities as "You can see a lot by looking") and an abundance of phrases that have slipped into our everyday language. Upon my return from a visit to Jamaica, I spent a class describing my travels and some of the words I learned while there such as "respect" (a greeting), "natty" (an adjective describing the dreadlocks or a greeting), and "spar" (friend). Though in twenty-two years I have heard a lot of trendy pop music from the students (and always from the boys some form of heavy metal or offshoot of punk rock), one constant has been each and every year there are youngsters who fall in love with their parents old Beatles and Bob Marley records or CDs. I can attest from personal experience to the truth that certain pieces of music transcend time and place and remain as powerful to later generations as they did to the first. Having visited Kingston and the Bob Marley Museum, and having seen firsthand the beauty and poverty of the island, I gained a better perspective of Marley's lyrics (and what he meant by terms such as screw face, bald head, and Sufferah). I also marveled at how positive he remained in his vision for a more enlightened world.

This leads me to the often maligned genre of writing called the *song lyric*. Since I myself write songs in my spare time, I tend to side with those who view lyric writing as a form of poetic expression if not what academics refer to as "pure poetry." Students who moan about assigned memorization of sonnets and the works of Robert Frost are often able to recite in full the words to their favorite songs and eagerly accept the challenge of writing their own song lyrics. Most often they use a familiar melody to write to, and in recent years students have tried their hand at writing in a rap or hip hop style. Once again the hardest part of this assignment is coming up with rhymes that are not forced or awkward or detract from the meaning of the lyric. Thus I don't have a specific assignment that requires students to write a song lyric. Instead I offer the option of writing in this format when we from time to time have free writing days. Always with this and other creative writing assignments I insist on *revision*. I am fully aware that for some talented individuals there are those moments of inspiration that can lead to almost fully realized pieces of work, but more often than not, writing is a process that includes revisiting your work and sharpening it—adding a word here, subtracting a word there, rephrasing a line, cutting out unnecessary words, rearranging lines. The earlier you get students to accept the need for applying revision to their writing, the better off they will be when crafting expository as well as creative writing as high schoolers and college students.

Two Birds with One Stone (Using Creative Writing to Teach Grammar and How to Use the Dictionary)

Creative writing for most students is the fun part of English class. Learning certain basics such as lessons on grammar or how to use a dictionary do not inspire a similar reaction. In fact, most students dread the very mention of the word "grammar", so why not devise methods to make such assignments or lessons more appealing? That was the idea behind the **Clauses Poem** exercise.

Every year in seventh grade I introduce the clause and explain the difference between a phrase and a clause (the latter has a subject and verb), the two types of clauses (independent and subordinate), and the three types of subordinate clauses, concentrating mostly on adjective and adverb clauses acting as modifiers. I believe that a dynamic teacher can make even the driest material interesting, but I for one fail miserably when it comes to instilling a love for grammar in my students. Yet I am also committed to teaching the craft of writing and believe that young writers should understand how and why we structure thoughts in sentences and then paragraphs and essays. Good communication depends upon clarity and thus the need to carefully explain the steps one takes to clearly narrate, explain or describe. At this stage in their development as writers my students have moved beyond writing a series of simple sentences to make a paragraph. Whether they know it or not they are writing complex sentences and using clauses, so I approach this lesson as the revealer. This is what you are doing now or can be doing, so let's look at it and pay attention to placement because where you put your phrases or clauses in the sentence matters. With Miss Gibb's mantra always in the back of my head ("When in doubt, take *Warriner's* out"), we practice identifying clauses in our grammar book, but then it is time to use clauses ourselves.

The **Clauses Poem** requires the students to write a non-rhyming piece of roughly twenty to twenty-four lines. I ask them to begin with an independent clause as the first line to be followed by a subordinate clause and then maintain that pattern. Of course, there are always a few students who wish to begin with a subordinate clause and as long as they can write and differentiate between subordinate and independent clauses, I let them deviate. For this assignment I ask the students to choose a member of their family. The clauses themselves must include specific imagery that they associate with their subject. For instance, if I were to write about my father I might focus on his love of sailing, and that conjures up in my mind certain smells of canvas and boat paint and his old Beetle. Thus I might begin:

My father used to love to sail
Which explains the smell of canvas in his patched-up VW bug
He loved the freedom of the open sea
After he had spent dull, gray weeks at the plant
Dad was a company man
Who gave thirty-five years of his life to Electric Boat
The plant made nuclear submarines
That were supposed to protect us from the Communists
On weekends Dad found refuge upon the cold Atlantic waters
Where he sailed beyond Napatree Point, around Fisher's Island, and as the sun set home again.

Again, stress using names of places, local expressions, anything that helps connect your piece to a time and place. Specific imagery always has more resonance.

Students obviously need to be able to use a dictionary which requires knowing where to find words and how to read the information, which includes part of speech, the roots, and often several definitions. The **Dictionary as Starting Point** assignment asks the students to find a page in the dictionary and read the words and their meanings. Next they are to choose ten to fifteen words and write a short *narrative* or *descriptive* piece of roughly one hundred and fifty to two hundred words. Ask them to avoid such vague words as "cool," "nice," and "great." I also suggest they be surreal or "nonsensible." I offer an example from page 304 of *Webster's Dictionary* (Watermill Press, 1991):

Paddy wagon, paean, pagan, pageantry, painting, paisley, palatable, palate, paleface, pajamas

*It was the **paisley pajamas** I remember most. Once bright colors dulled by years of detergent softeners and spin cycles. The threadbare pj's clung to his weathered body like the last of autumn's leaves. His face was rough and sun-dried, not unlike one of those characters in a Winslow Homer **painting**....*

Students can and often do show off their sense of humor on such assignments which is an effective outlet in an otherwise serious-minded, structured regimen. But this assignment also forces students to return to a very valuable source that cannot be overestimated, the good old dictionary. I often remind my students, "Don't leave home without it."

Speaking of home, we now come to the **Special Place** writing assignment. I have stuck with this assignment for a good number of years now because being able to describe and capture the essence of a place (be it a cove or a town or a region or even one's room) is the well-covered territory of both prose writers and poets. And this is where the lines between creative writing and expository writing blur for me, and I see them as having much more in common with one another than those who like to separate the two will ever admit. Expository writing is when you convey information and "explain what is difficult to understand." Some years back a student of mine did just that in a creative piece about her birthplace, New Zealand.

New Zealand

New Zealand
A place of wonderful baby books,
first teeth and my family, especially
my grandfather.
Building castles out of black
Sand, taking my first steps.
Steps that would eventually take
Me to a plane and fly me 13,000
Miles away,
Away from my family.
Away from everything I knew and
Loved.
But these steps also take me on a
Plane to fly back.
When I return I walk through a
Maze of memories,
Some old, some new, many lost.
I feel sad seeing old toys or stuffed
Animals because I know I had
Such fun with them, but I can't

Remember it.

A place of happiness gone forever,
Just like my grandfather.
In many ways New Zealand is a happy
And wonderful place filled with family and friends, but
There will always be a sadness there,
Waiting for me.

There are many fine things happening in this work—the use of *alliteration* effective and unforced, the sense of movement conveyed (both physical and emotional), the conflict she accepts and the longing for what can never be again is palpable. You feel what this young writer has gone through, so for me it's very good creative writing. It also conveys something that is difficult to understand and therefore fits the definition of expository writing. But let's dispense with these terms and simply marvel at the work itself. Good writing period conveys what is difficult to understand and a young girl named Katherine did so when she was thirteen years old.

For this assignment I ask the students to think of a place that is special. It may be a room in their house, a section of a city, a lake the family visits, a tree in the backyard, a ballpark, a theatre, a country. Then I ask them to think about what makes the place special. What reminds them of that place? What feelings do they associate with that place? What sights, sounds and smells do they connect with that place? Again I ask my students not to rhyme but to use specific imagery. I instruct them to convey a clear tone and mood. I use Katherine's piece and several others from former students to give them some ideas (and to show them that other students have successfully tackled this assignment). I suggest between fifteen and thirty lines, but I also note that "less is often more" and share with them a piece by a boy named Max:

Candles guide me through a blanket of incense
toward the repeating sounds of Disc-O-Rama
Gazing at the shapes floating in my head
From the posters of my idols I realize
I am alone in my room and in the world
I am myself and no one can change me
I can only guide myself aimlessly through my life

That is all one should be expected to do
Lead yourself alone.

"Lead yourself alone." Quite a statement of independence. Young people can be very provocative if given the opportunity and prodded to push themselves. Teachers need what George Will likes to refer to as "equipoise," a balance of conflicting strengths. You want to give students freedom, but with direction, a wide range of possible topics, but with the understanding that the student must hone in on one specific topic or aspect of the topic. You want to give them enough time, but also set deadlines. You want to allow them freedom of expression, but only if they understand the degree of responsibility that goes with it. You want them to question authority (or at least I do), but politely. You've got to have "equipoise."

It's Alive—The Use of Personification

Teaching what poetry really is requires a hands-on approach. That is, make young people write poetry as you study it. Students can read a poem rich in alliteration, simile and sound images such as Dylan Thomas's "Fern Hill" (aloud, always aloud), and you can perhaps instill an appreciation in them for such mastery of poetic devises, but especially children in elementary and middle school need to do it for themselves to gain a truly genuine understanding and respect for such means of expression. *Personification*, in particular, is a fairly straightforward concept and easily applicable to writing assignments for this age group. I call this assignment **"It's Alive"** and ask the students to imagine a situation at home or at school where an appliance or inanimate object comes alive and causes havoc. Students have written about ballistic pencil sharpeners, the battle of Mr. Toaster and Mrs. Refrigerator, talking alphabet soup, a rogue soccer ball. Students tend to really enjoy writing what Mark Twain might have referred to as "real stretchers," and they then want to read them to the rest of the class. An amazing thing happens from time to time. When I hear the student read the piece aloud I sometimes experience the piece in a new way and gain a better appreciation of what the young writer was trying to convey. Other amazing things happen, such as shy students being encouraged to read and then experiencing the support of their peers. Sometimes the students critique one another's work (always with gentle guidance and stressing the importance to carefully choose our words when pointing out flaws). At other times one student's piece can lead the others to suggest their own endings or alternative ideas and once again we may be on an unexpected detour that reveals the wonderful world of children's imagination.

3

Art For Writing's Sake

As you can probably tell by now, I like to impress upon my students the idea that certain types of writing should be considered art. Certainly poetry and song lyrics and prose that's not formulaic and script writing measure up to any definition of art. *Webster's Seventh New Collegiate Dictionary* has twelve definitions of the word including one handy, all-purpose one that I like which reads, "The conscious use of skill, taste, and creative imagination in the production of aesthetic objects or works so produced." Of course we also think of drawing, painting and sculpture or what students are typically exposed to in art class. I tell them immediately that creative writing is a type of art and that both their art teacher and I seek to train them to be good observationists, interpreters, and experimenters.

To solidify the connection between art and writing, I have introduced at varying times three writing assignments. The first is called the **Painting Poem** exercise. I ask the students to first find a painting either in a book or at a museum or even hanging on a wall at home. He or she is to study the painting and consider why the artist chose that subject matter, the colors, the angle or perspective, and then consider what the artist was trying to say with the painting. Now the students have a choice. They can write a poem which details the imagery in words and concludes with a statement (the message or point of the painting). Some students love the idea of using words to paint a picture. One year a boy named Peter tackled a Claude Monet painting in what he titled *The Rouen Cathedral, West Façade, Sunlight.*

> *Shadows,*
> *Blurred and faded,*
> *Crowd the facility in dark,*
> *Lazy sloths*
> *Of blue.*

As seen through an artist's eye,
Forty canvasses of dawn and dusk,
Light and dark,
Echo reality
And abstractness.

As seen through an artist's eye,
The arches are engulfed
In a bright luminescence
From the world of canvas.

Light is the subject.
Not the building,
Nor the people,
But the late morning sun,
Swallowing the tower
In a yellow mist of brightness.

Heaven knows what preceded this.
A sun shower,
A cold morning,
Or an average day.

And there is no way to tell
What is yet to come.
Hazy afternoon,
Frost-bitten twilight,
Or a warm evening.

Now Peter was an amazingly talented eleven-year-old who seemed to always be inspired by such writing assignments. Other students are often more tentative, and for them I offer the choice of writing a short essay that again details what is happening in the painting. They are to conclude their essay with an interpretation of what they think the artist was trying to point out about the subject. I also suggest to them that they may want to tell me what they think the painting reveals about the artist. Both assignments help show students that writers need to be keen observers and looking at art is a good way to convey this idea. Remember what Yogi Berra said. "You can see a lot by looking."

The next assignment I call the **Color Poem**. Painters use color to express emotions, create moods, signal warning, communicate ideas. Writers are word painters who use color with equal measure. Different colors represent a variety of ideas and feelings, and we associate many moods and life moments with colors. This assignment requires the student to choose a color of interest and to write a creative piece that captures the essence of the color. What does the color make you think of? What does the color often symbolize in works of art? How do other people use that color? What phrases or quotes does the color remind us of? I offer two examples of my own.

Brown

Brown is an earthy color
Mud, mulch, dirt, leaves in autumn, bark

Brown are my dog's eyes
Pleading, loving, begging, forgiving

Brown is my baseball mitt,
Root beer, the Godfather of Soul,
The color of a jazzman's fingers
Wrapped around a golden trumpet

Brown is as American as the red, white and
Blues.

Brown is everywhere.

Green

Green bursts forth
In ballparks and schoolyards,
The aftermath of April showers,
The answer to a farmer's prayers.

Green thumbs poke the moist soil
Where worms work and new growth awakes.

"The kid's green," the old manager
spits, "but he's got promise."
The pitcher snaps his arm and the bat cracks back
A bounding promise to keep.

"I'm envious of you," a mother
muses watching her daughter walk gingerly
cloaked in a light drizzle,
her eyes wide open.

In these pieces I try to introduce *alliteration* and *assonance* and associating expressions with words and color. No, this is not great poetry, but I use it to remind the students to write from their passions and to show them that I, too, write. I am not asking them to do something I haven't tried my hand at. W.D. Snodgrass once said, "Very few people at any one time ever write poetry that is any good. But surely all of them will read it and teach it with greater sympathy and understanding for having tried to write some." I agree.

The third assignment is the **Stream of Consciousness** exercise. I connect this to art in that stream of consciousness writing is very impressionistic and reminds me of Jackson Pollack (or Jack the Dripper) who splashed paints onto large canvases that definitely left an impression on people. I do not go into great detail with my Seventh Graders about James Joyce or Marcel Proust or Jack Kerouac, but I do introduce them to stream of consciousness writing because it is a good exercise in training young people to free associate and hopefully discover the connectedness of past and present, dream and memory, people and places. Sometimes I even allow the students to talk while doing this so that anything said aloud might trigger an association that leads to something else. "What's the point?" someone always asks. A good answer might be, "Who knows?" or "Let's find out."

Writing is so often a journey without a designated or certain end point. It's a quest, a search for "what's the point?" Hopefully my students learn that from this and other exercises.

Bumping

I have always been amazed at how some artists are able to collaborate on a piece, while others find it difficult if not impossible to work with another person. Similarly, each year I have certain students who want to work with each other in groups, yet there are always a few who balk at the idea. Being able to work with other people and contribute constructively to a collective are important life skills, and therefore writing assignments that allow for such involvement are beneficial. Over the years my students have gotten in groups to make movies, hold debates, and create poems out of the store bought **Magna Poetry** kits. I have also assigned them to work in pairs on what I call the **Bumping** story. Often youngsters in my fifth grade class, when asked to read aloud, inquire if they can "bump" to someone else instead of me dictating who reads when and for how long. So for this activity I group the class in pairs and give each group a picture as a starting point. A wonderful collection of illustrations to use for this is the portfolio edition of *The Mysteries of Harris Burdick* by Chris Van Allsburg. Other good sources are photographs from *Life* magazine or *National Geographic*. After discussing the picture and what kind of story they want to write, one student writes down the opening sentence or two. Then the other student responds, and from there they continue writing the story over the course of several class periods. I do not require that each student write the exact same number of sentences, but I do stress that they need to equally distribute the work load so that it is a true collaboration. Ideally, this also helps the students with the editing process, but truth be told, appreciating the importance of editing is a taste most thirteen-year-olds have not yet acquired. Still, many students truly enjoy this opportunity to work on creating a story with a classmate.

Portrait in Words

For the **Student Portrait** assignment I also pair up students, but this time each writes separately about the other person. The required format recently has been a minimum of three paragraphs with the preference being five paragraphs including an introduction (when I first met this person) and a conclusion. I give the students leeway as far as what they write about in the three middle paragraphs while suggesting ideas such as personality, physical appearance, character traits, habits, hobbies, ways that person has changed or stayed the same. I tell them they may wish to write about how others perceive that person. I implore them to be honest but also sensitive to the fact that some people are better equipped or better tempered to handle such honesty. There is a difference between gently poking fun of someone and intentionally being cruel, but even more so I remind myself of what Dr. Mel Levine pointed out: "Kids don't always know how what they say or how they say it comes across." We as teachers deal with this all the time. I believe my job is to get students to be more open and honest, but I must also stress the need for empathy and a vigilant awareness of others' feelings. The portrait assignment tests my judgment in selecting people to write about one another as it challenges students to write honestly, but not hurtfully.

One of the girls in a recent seventh grade class wrote of the boy she was assigned, "He often sports an impish grin that reveals most of his teeth. He comes across as having a nonchalant feeling when it comes to life and those around him, yet his views on school are much like my own: study hard, do well, a no-nonsense attitude. He believes in working hard and sleeping in." Later she adds, "He'll tell a story like you wouldn't believe. He'll jazz it up every which way so that by the end of it, even if you were there, you don't know what's true. But it won't matter because it sure did cause some excitement in the room." This is good clean writing and zeroes in on how the boy presents himself to his friends contrasting with his very serious approach to school work. She also rightfully mentions his skill as a storyteller, and when I read this I nodded in agreement. In many a class this boy would tell the funniest, often even surreal stories about what he saw happen over the weekend either at a friend's house or while out in public at the movies or mall. In turn, the boy wrote of the girl when they were in the lower grades, "When we would gather in the mornings and talk, she would seem to be having more fun preparing for the day and getting a head start on everything while we were just goofing around. She seemed more conscientious than the rest of us. We would make friends and the other people we didn't like we would just stay out of their business and they would just do the same. She would always seem to be friends with everyone, never treating anyone how she wouldn't like to be treated." A bit later on he added, "She also seemed too mature for her age by always thinking things through before doing them. She would think of the consequences and repercussions." As you can see, quite a lot of thought went into this piece. Not that all of the compositions reveal such insight and effort. But you read a piece such as this and tell yourself, "Some of them are really listening."

Dr. Seuss and the Comic Book

Most of my students love to draw funny characters, especially on my chalk board in the morning before the day officially begins. I encourage it. In fact, I tell the students it's okay to doodle in their notebooks as long as they are doing well on their quizzes for me. One year I had an incredibly talented youngster make the most amazing doodle of a creature with over a hundred heads, all with different expressions.

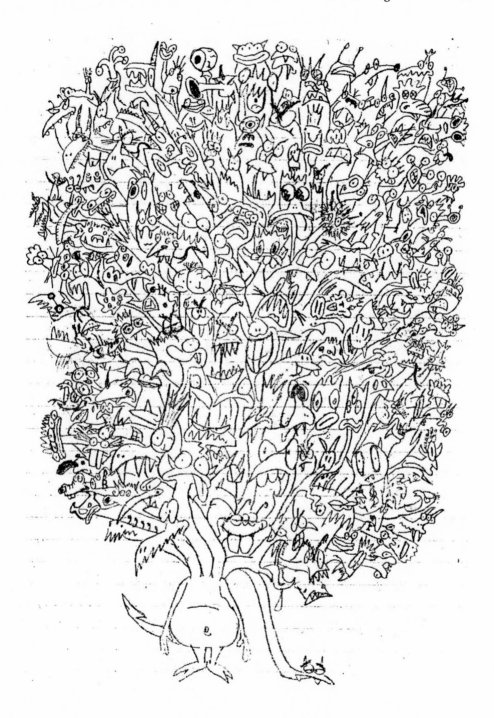

He did this during English classes yet always knew what page we were on and never scored below a 90 on any of his various quizzes in grammar, vocabulary and reading. So why not let him doodle? I also offer students the opportunity to illustrate their stories, poems, even essays if they are so inclined to do so. Sometimes drawing the pictures helps the student get ideas for (or go back and add to) the writing.

I also discovered at one point that older students in middle school still love the Dr. Seuss stories they read as younger people. The stories, the humor, the illustrations, the funny-sounding words all resonate with "kids" of any age. That said, I did not come up with the idea of asking my students to write a story in the style of Dr. Seuss. Like many of my most successful writing projects, this one was suggested by a student. I had taught Jason in fifth grade and discovered two things about him. He was a very articulate youth with an excellent grasp of vocabulary and a fertile imagination, but he also struggled when trying to use those gifts in his writing. When he reached seventh grade, his mom voiced concerns about his lack of motivation and development as a writer. Later she approached me again with a question. Jason loved Dr. Seuss and was actually working on his own Seussian story. Would it be okay if he submitted it as a writing assignment? Not only was it okay, but I thought it would be a fun challenge for all of the students in seventh grade. Thus was born the Dr. Seuss story writing assignment, and every year I use Jason's story as a model, not only because it genuinely captures the tone and feel of a Dr. Seuss story, but also because it represents the story of Jason (a good bit of motivation for other youngsters who struggle with writing). I think it's safe to say Jason floundered and avoided creative writing as much as possible for a year and half in my classes until he found the right format to launch his imagination and present his skills. That is why each year I try to offer a wide variety of assignments and exercises and am always looking for new ones. But Jason's story also reminds us that young people sometimes know what works, and you have to allow them that opportunity. "Follow the child," as Dr. Montessori suggested. Following Jason led us to the brilliance of "The Speediest Zeed."

Now listen to a story of Wankle O'Zeed,
like all other Zeeds Wankle loved to speed.

He'd get into his revedee rever and vroom,
He'd be gone all of the day and afternoon.

He'd race all the other Zeeds and beat all
    except one.
He said, "Why should little boy Webster have
 all of the fun?"

You see little boy Webster's stoketee stact
could beat any revedee rever and that's just a
            fact.

"How can I beat him?" Wankle would
     mutter and glitch.
"Yes, I know I could beat him with a tumbalee
     tich.
A tumbalee tich tumbles so fast and it tilts;
 It's the fastest machine that's ever
     been built."

 So Wankle went to the maker of tumbalee tich
and said, "Sir, how much must I give you to take home with me
     this?"
 The maker looked down and said with a sigh,
"Give me seventeen pennies and a crushed clamshell pie."

 Wankle searched through his pockets and said with a
     snort,
"I do have the pie but am two pennies
     short."

 "You have a deal," the maker he said.
So Wankle tumbled away and painted
     it red.

The next day Wankle won but not by an
     extreme.
He said, "I need more speed for Webster I must
     cream.

I want to embarrass him and make him say
that I could beat him anywhere any day."

So Wankle bought a brand new engine,
a trivelee triff
and renamed his machine the Tumbling
Shniff.
He knew he could win; there would be no
contest,
And all of the Zeeds would know that
he sped the best.

The next day when he raced,
Wankle swooshed as fast as he could go;
He was moving so quick he made Webster look
slow.

To the Zeeds it was like a dream,
so fast and so clean;
There was only one problem; Wankle couldn't stop
his machine.

He knew he shouldn't have shown off for his
Tumbling Shniff
Rolled right through the town and went
over the cliff.

It's been twenty-five years since anyone
has seen Wankle O'Zeed
Who today is known to have sped the
fastest speed.
But sometimes late at night the Zeeds hear
him say,
"I had to be the best by a long shot
and look where I am today."

I remember marveling at how Jason created his own language, used *onomato-poeia*, carefully constructed a story line and in the end showed us the potential consequences of greed. Though he may have asked for some help on a few of the rhymes, there is too much "kid sense" and kid expressions for this not to be his. Students often question authorship when they hear or read another student's work that seems to stand out from their other work. As a teacher I have occasionally had to deal with the issue of parental help. In this case so much of this reflects Jason's personality and sense of humor (the bit about the pennies) and his confidence that he always exuded except when writing. It was a major breakthrough for him and provided me with a wonderful model and new writing assignment. I am forever grateful to you, "Dr. Ed."

These days I assign this project to my fifth grade class. I ask them to think of a funny situation or a family experience, maybe a conflict between two people, an interesting news event, a hobby such as fishing or horseback riding. Then I ask them to make up an imaginary place. Think up some characters with funny made-up names. Next they need to think of how to tell the story simply, rhyming if possible, but not a requirement. They must also draw their own pictures and color them in. I suggest they add as much detail to the drawings as they can think of. As examples, I read to them from various Dr. Seuss stories. *The Lorax*, in particular, has excellent examples of made-up characters (Once-ler, humming fish, Brown Bar-ba-loots), setting (the street of the lifted Lorax where the Grickle-grass grows), and those wonderfully zany made-up inventions, nouns, verbs and adjectives such as "whisper-ma-phone," 'super ax-hacker," "snargled," "snergelly" and "smogulous" to name a few.

I also recommend that students seek inspiration by going to the library and reading Dr. Seuss books, and we take turns reading some aloud in class to hear the way the author uses the sound of language to help convey his story. Meanwhile, we also discuss the fine line between using parts of ideas from a story as a starting point verses taking someone else's idea completely and calling it your own (i.e. *plagiarism*). Now I love Yeats' quote that "bad artists borrow, great artists steal" and original ideas may indeed be hard to come by, but we have a responsibility as teachers to clearly impress upon our young charges what is acceptable usage of another's work and what is not. There is a difference between referencing another's work and using that work as if it were your own. This gets more and more complicated in the Internet age when so much information and ideas are available to students, but I do encourage my older students to ransack the culture for ideas for their stories as long as they cite their sources (lessons in *footnotes* and *bibliography* should be required in all disciplines by fifth or sixth grade). Sometimes we discuss how this is done in movies and songs, and I show examples of where credit is given to the original artists.

The other longer writing assignment that requires illustrations is the **Comic Book.** Similar to the **Dr. Seuss** project, I usually allow students several weeks to complete this assignment. In preparation for it we practice drawing from scratch several types of cartoon characters (an animal with human characteristics, a superhero, a Simpsons-type funny character). I show them several comics and suggest they bring some in from home or ask their parents to take them out to buy some comics. We have to research this genre and look at how this type of writing successfully presents a story. We talk about panels, captions, dialogue balloons, the use of *onomatopoeia*, drawing action sequences, the importance of using words and pictures together to tell the story, the language of comics including identifiable phrases, the proper tools, how to use the computer to create panels and dialogue balloons, and using color to create *tone* and *mood*. An excellent text to use is Michael Morgan Pellowski's *The Art of Making Comic Books.*

An offshoot of the **Comic book** project is the **Superhero** story. For this assignment I ask each student to invent a superhero for our times. This individual should have a catchy name, a costume, and at least one super power. Next I suggest the following. Devise a story in which the superhero has to save the day. The story needs a villain who presents a problem that needs to be solved. Think about and include a description of where and when the story takes place. I ask my students to think about sequence. That is, the story must have a beginning, middle, and end. It might begin with an introduction of the villain doing some evil deed to be followed by an introduction of the superhero who must somehow learn of what is happening and then determine to come to the rescue. I add that it always helps to explain motive and give background information. Why is the villain plotting to cause harm to others? How did your superhero come to be? Why does he go out of his way to fight crime? Of course the confrontation or battle is central to the story. Here the writer can have some fun describing the super powers of both hero and villain. I also insist that the story not end with the tag line "To be continued." That is too easy. Conclude the story with a sense of uncertainty or mystery, but conclude it none the less.

For the **Superhero** story I give the students the option of adding illustrations. Sometimes instead I ask them to simply draw a picture of their super hero or a scene from the story as their cover. I also make it very clear to them that of all of these assignments that include drawing, I am most interested in the writing itself, the story, the thought that went into its development and content. Regarding the drawing I ask the students to be neat with their coloring and to add as much detail to the pictures and it's that detail I look for, not the student's drawing skills.

I must end this chapter with the work of one of my students from some years back. He was the doodler who quietly drew pictures in the back row, yet always knew where we were in the lesson. Preston was part of a talented class which included three superstar math whizzes, a child prodigy violin player, a girl whose writing inspired me to come up with more challenging writing assignments, a fantastic lacrosse player who also happened to enjoy writing, one of the greatest chortlers I've ever met, an extraordinary girl whose athletic skills suggested pure natural ability, a quiet boy who claimed he did not like to write but by his senior year was writing thoughtful, funny pieces, and this often bemused cartoon artist whose work shall long be remembered at our school. He was also a very capable writer, and he put the two skills together to produce "Where Have All the Dinosaurs Gone?"

A long, long, long, long
time ago dinosaurs did rule.
They wallowed in primordial slime,
and it was really cool!

But then one day they disappeared
and no one knows quite why
That one day these humongous beasts
just all of the sudden died.

Maybe a volcano blew
and lava poured from its spout,
or maybe it was climate change
that made them all die out.

Maybe they were really, really,
really heavy smokers.
Maybe they lost all their money
in a game of poker.

Maybe they drank too much water
and they had to go,
but all the bathrooms were out of order
and they did explode.

Maybe they read too many books
and they got eye strain
or maybe they held metal rods
in lightning storms and rain.

Maybe they ate lots of rocks
mistaking them for food
or maybe they never bathed
and the smell became too crude.

Or maybe they could have died of boredom
on a rainy day.
Maybe they all burnt their hands
while grilling a fillet.

Maybe they were meant to die
and meant to go away.
Maybe some of them survived
and live this very day!

They may be in your neighborhood
or walking down the street.
So just beware of people
with tails and scaly feet.

It's important to allow students the opportunity to utilize their sense of humor, and in encouraging it I have often ended up deterring into discussions about what is appropriate material in student writing. Here the "bathroom humor" was presented in a clever, humorous way which I deemed acceptable. Young people love to test boundaries and see how the adult is going to react. Seventh graders often ask me if they can use expletives in their writing, and I usually reply that the frequently used cuss words are common and vulgar and suggest that instead they make up their own words that represent or replace the overused ones. Again, a careful discussion of the origins of the words in question may help students better understand why such words are frowned upon. My father used to sail and he sure could swear like a sailor, so I am accustomed to and personally not offended as much as others by such words. I sometimes use them myself as anyone who has ever golfed with me will attest. Such taboos are always attractive to young teens. For many, using swear words is a rite of passage, a badge of independence as immortalized by Mark Twain's Huckleberry Finn. Yet today's pop culture has oversaturated the airwaves with a redundant and repulsive overuse of four-letter words so, as a reaction, I am recently less nonchalant about their occasional appearance in student writing.

Ah, I'm getting ahead of myself. The power of words is coming up in the next chapter. For now I need to bid adieu to the art chapter with one last thought. Let the students doodle. If it's a question of distraction, set aside some time each week for the doodlers to express themselves. Who knows what fantastic ideas may emerge from such scratch work?

4

Points of Departure

When I was born I was black.
When I grew up I was black.
When I got sick I was black.
When I go outside in the sun I am black.
When I die I'll be black.

But you

When you were born you were pink.
When you grew up you were white.
When you got sick you were blue.
When you go out in the sun you are red.
When you die you will be purple.

And you have the nerve to call me "colored."

One inauspicious day in April 1990, a young girl named Marisa brought this poem to my attention. She was excited to share it with me and the class because she had made that magical discovery of how words strung together can be so powerful. She wrote it down, having heard it from a friend and told us it was by "anynoumos" which led us to discuss what *anonymous* means. Since we had been doing weekly dictations, mostly of poems, Marisa suggested I include this in future lessons, and I have used it ever since. It provides us the opportunity to discuss how one simple line or sentence can speak volumes if presented in the right context or set up well. We talk about the term "colored" and the unjust restrictions and attitudes associated with the Jim Crow laws that were present in south Florida right up to the early 1960's. I introduce and discard dictation pieces all the time, but I keep using this one because it never fails to make its point felt. It also introduces the idea that writing can be used to address social ills and injustice. Writing should provoke thought, discussion, even action.

A year or so later, a group of seventh graders asked me if we could read Harper Lee's *To Kill A Mockingbird*. After consideration and consultation with the department head, I agreed and tried to help them untangle the knot of family history that takes up the first part of the novel. Of course, the students loved the episodes with Boo Radley and then the central story of Tom Robinson and Atticus Finch's noble efforts to defend him. Once again students were confronted with the subject of prejudice and the injustice of a racist system. This book continues to have the power to move young people to say, "This is wrong. This should not happen." In these situations I keep my views and comments to a minimum and simply let the students react and respond to one another. Students also must read as Scout asks, "Atticus, do you defend niggers?" His reply is so unruffled yet forceful, full of "equipoise." He admonishes her not to use such terms and explains that it is his job to help Tom and if he shirked his responsibility, he couldn't ask his children to do something and expect them to do it. There is so much to learn from such passages, lessons that remain just as relevant today.

The term "nigger" incites a variety of responses as one could imagine. Some students refuse to say the offensive word aloud which is admirable. Other students consider it akin to swearing and raise their voices when reading it so that the sensitive ones clearly hear it. Others say it doesn't mean as much anymore because you hear it in movies and on music videos and CDs now, and someone always reminds us that African-Americans use it all the time which leads to another opportunity to discuss the power of words and who gives them such power. Context, again, is everything. I tell the students how my Italian father-in-law uses the term "guinea" from time to time, but that if I used the term it may sound more derogatory coming from me since I'm what Mr. deLilla affectionately calls a "whitie." If African-Americans use the term "nigger" they are in a sense taking the word back, redefining it, changing its meaning and usage. Perhaps the controversial comedian Lenny Bruce was onto something when he suggested that suppression of the word is what gives it its power to hurt. My point is that where, when, why and how a word is used as well as who is using it affects its meaning. Students enjoy these discussions and being able to voice their formative ideas and views. Let it happen. This is where humanistic learning takes place.

Students need to become sensitive to and aware of the connotation as well as denotation of words. I am occasionally reminded by students that I too need to be on my toes when using terms. I once told a group of students not to call a boy in their class a "dwarf" because dwarves and giants were "freaks of nature." Now, of course, the students turned it around and suggested I was calling the boy a freak. I became defensive and pulled out the dictionary and attempted to explain that the word "freak" could mean "unusual or abnormal" and that dwarves and giants were thus not the norm but "freaks of nature." I meant well but, at least it's been my experience that as soon as you get defensive, students sense a moment of weakness and pounce. It did lead to a class lecture disguised as discussion on all that I have mentioned in this chapter. But in time I saw their point. The boy was short, so they affectionately called him "dwarf," but they would never call him a "freak." "Mr. Winans, a freak is a weirdo, you know, someone who is crazy. We wouldn't call our friend a freak." So now I was being taught about connotation. The boys had to nail home the point by calling each other a "freak" whenever someone did or said something strange and were within earshot of the teacher. I get it, guys.

I think it is safe to say a majority of my students have been taught at home as well as at school not to judge a person based on skin color. I wish I could say the same in regards to judging people based on sexuality. I have several times reprimanded students for calling classmates "fags" or telling jokes that bash gay people. I again draw their attention to how much words can resonate and help to pick people up or put them down. I know I have benefited from having gay friends recount stories of growing up knowing who they are, but not being able to say, fearing ridicule, aware of perhaps never escaping people's narrow-minded judgment. I want to believe we can all evolve to the point where we accept one another's differences just as we embrace our similarities. For now as a teacher I offer vignettes and ask my students to think about what they've heard or read. Think about how this individual feels. Getting young people to think about and feel for others leads to better understanding and, hopefully, ultimately, acceptance.

Thursday Chapel Sept. 12, 2002 "Mr. Robinson & The Fiddler's Dream"

(Note: The following is the text of a chapel presentation/musical performance I gave one morning to our upper schoolers.)

Back in the mid-1980's a man by the name of Peter Robinson arrived at Gulf Stream to teach music and English. He was a Midwesterner in all the best ways, open-minded, always friendly, a good listener. In the dedication to him in the yearbook (*Mariner XVII*) it reads, "We do admire his arts-playing the piano beautifully, writing music of his own, preserving by teaching tunes to 'little ones' a corpus of dying folk tunes, respecting the contemporary, tolerating the modern, and revering the Romantic and Classical composers. We listen because he listens; we sing because he lightens our hearts and respects our voices; we grow because he keeps growing. We desire his arts." Mr. Robinson was also an inspired English teacher, a better one than I was, but I couldn't be jealous of him. How can you be jealous of a good person? Mr. Robinson once made me a tape from his vast record collection. On it were several songs by a bluegrass musician and songwriter named John Hartford. This tickled me because as a child I used to watch *The Glen Campbell Goodtime Hour* on television, on which John Hartford was a regular musical guest. He had written a hit song "Gentle On My Mind" for Glen Campbell and also appeared weekly on the number one rated television show, *The Smother Brothers Comedy Hour*. After this brief brush with fame, Mr. Hartford fulfilled a childhood dream by studying for and attaining his steamboat pilot license. It just so happened that as a boy in St. Louis, John's passion to become a steamboat pilot was stirred by his fifth grade teacher who gave him some books on the subject. In his tribute to her, "Mrs. Ferris," Mr. Hartford sings

Me oh my, how the time does fly!
The time and the river keep a-rollin' on by.
Now I'm not a student and she's not a teacher.
But we both still love the Mississippi River, uh-huh.

I like the idea that someone wrote a song about his fifth grade teacher. Mr. Hartford never gave up music. He made dozens of records, toured the country many times, and was a musical consultant for the movie *O Brother, Where Are Thou?* before passing away last year. There has been a real revival of bluegrass and old timey music since the success of the *O Brother* soundtrack. A few weeks ago I bought a John Hartford CD and came across a good quote that reminded me of Mr. Robinson when it described John Hartford as understanding that "tradition isn't something you blindly obey, it's fuel for the future."

The movie *O Brother, Where Art Thou?* not only revitalized much of the American public's interest in traditional music, it also set Homer's epic, *The Odyssey*, in a more modern context, Depression-era America. Early in the film the three main characters, Ulysses Everett McGill, Delmar and Pete, escape the chain gang at Parchman's Farm, which is a very real place, a notoriously harsh prison camp in the deep South. This caught my attention because some years back I had heard and become enamored of a singer named Ted Hawkins who, I was to learn, had actually served time at Parchman's Farm. Ted lived a very difficult life as a modern-day wandering minstrel who spent many years singing for his supper on street corners, in particular the boardwalk out in Venice Beach, California. He had a voice that mesmerized me: tender one moment, anguished the next. So I wrote a lyric about him I called "Terror and Love." This happened at around the time I was working on a song about Huck Finn. The Eighth Graders may remember reciting those words about Finn for a chapel with me when they were in fifth grade. The Eights may also recall pestering me to play my "gee-tar" for them in fifth grade and then again last year in seventh grade. I resisted but absent-mindedly, half-heartedly semi-promised them I would do so during the year, but I (a-hem) "chickened out." However, now that I am doing a chapel that started out being about Peter Robinson who re-introduced me to the music of John Hartford who was a musical contributor to *O Brother, Where Art Thou?* which opens up with a scene of Parchman's Farm, well, I figured I'd play you my song about Ted Hawkins. But then I went back to that song lyric about Huck Finn and thought it would be neat to figure out some simple music for it and play "Finn" for the Eights and the rest of you, but nothing came to me sooooo I thought about this being a chapel about John Hartford and how John Hartford being a steamboat captain who had worked on the Mississippi River once titled one of his records *Mark Twang* and being that Mr. Hartford had passed away recently and deserved a tribute of some sort, well...I ended up writing a little song about John Hartford and incorporated some of the lyrics from the Finn song in it so Eights, you may remember some of the lines here. This is called "Fiddle Me A River." Besides being a very competent guitar player, Mr. Hartford also played banjo, mandolin, and fiddle. This is for Mr. Hartford and his fifth grade teacher, Mrs. Ferris.

John John the steamboat's gone but bless my soul the river rolls on
Around the creek up past the bend where everything old is new again

Slap that fiddle play that lick blow your horn when the fog gets thick
Remember how Huck helped his friend Jim; I'd like to think I would have done like him

There's a hard luck story everywhere you go and river towns full of do-si-do
And when the law's wrong it ain't no sin to help a man find his family again

John John the steamboat's gone but bless my soul the river rolls on

Every generation's got its Kings and Dukes, senseless crazy family feuds
Poets and singers who soothe the soul and warm you up when the wind blows cold

And kids who dream of river boats and don't mind puttin' on hand-me down clothes
Old men skipping in the morning dew kicking up dust as you fiddle a tune

So who's that sittin' on the porch tonight singing high and lonesome in the blue moon light
Must be the ghost of ol' Huck Finn everything old is new again

John John the steamboat's gone but bless my soul the river rolls on

I suddenly got the idea to include this text and lyric from one of my chapel presentations because it ties into the idea of "points of departure." Every year teachers at my school are asked to give a talk or read a passage or present a slide show once or twice during the school year. A part of me dreads the prospect of doing this, but another part of me considers it a challenge to come up with something different and original. I often use musicians as a focal point because their stories are so interesting and, in my spare time, I have read and studied the lives of as well as the work of songwriters such as Woody Guthrie, Bob Dylan, Van Morrison, Bob Marley, Patti Smith, and Chuck Berry. I also love showing young people the connectedness of people and places, the recurrence of themes, and the importance of those who came before. When I learned of John Hartford's passing, I said to myself, "We need to remember this man. He carried on the tradition of bluegrass and added a wonderful sense of humor to it." I also thought of my former colleague Peter Robinson, so I played this old tape he had given me and upon hearing the song to Mrs. Ferris, I started to formulate some ideas for my chapel talk. I also kept in mind those students who wanted to hear me play my guitar and suddenly things came together. John Hartford the steamboat captain, Mark Twain and the Mississippi River, the old lyric about Huck Finn could all be tied together. The idea that Mr. Hartford followed his dream and was inspired by his fifth grade teacher shouted at me, "Dave, good story to relate to your students."

The chapel was a success but not so the follow up later in the year when I determined to have my seventh graders read *The Adventures of Huckleberry Finn*. A teacher's year can be measured in multitudes of daily successes and failures. My attempt to show the Sevens the ongoing relevance of Twain's classic story of the runaway boy who determines to help his friend escape to freedom and by doing so break the law of the times was merited but not well-executed. It was challenging reading and a number of students did improve their skill at deciphering Twain's various dialects, but only a few of the students got swept into the story. Perhaps they will come to appreciate the story more when they are older and reintroduced to it. As for myself, I will have to re-approach the story and how best to present the proper context for it the next time we read it. You know there will be a next time.

To Kill A Mockingbird and *The Adventures of Huckleberry Finn* reflect periods of time in our history that we must study, understand, and never forget. These are also complex stories which portray people not as caricatures or one-dimensional. We cannot simplify history or people; it is, as James Carville once described democracy, "a messy business." As Atticus Finch reminds us, we must consider Mayella Ewell's perspective and motives to better understand her. Over the years most of my better writers have been voracious readers, and these are the types of books that make us examine ourselves.

The Magnificence of *Maniac Magee*

I am always on the lookout for books that don't talk down to kids but do speak to them. One such author is Jerry Spinelli whose work clearly indicates that he remembers quite well what goes on in a young person's head. He has written several books I cannot recommend enough, including *Stargirl* and *Loser* in recent years. However, his masterpiece remains *Maniac Magee*, a book suggested to me by a former colleague who was curious to know what I thought of the novel's unvarnished look at race relations. Parts of the story are unflinching in their depiction of bleakness (Grayson's unattended funeral), poverty and ignorance (the cockroach-infested McNab household where they are building a pillbox to defend themselves against the blacks), the realities of homelessness (Maniac sleeps in the zoo and eats scraps left for the animals), and the resentment of many members of the black community (represented by MarsBar and the old man who call Maniac "Fishbelly" and "Whitie"). Yet it is also filled with joyful moments (Maniac's Christmas with Grayson, his time with the Beales playing in opened fire hydrants and singing at church), incredible triumphs (Maniac helping Grayson the illiterate old man learn to read, coaxing the little Beales to take a bath, convincing the McNab twins to go to school, untying Cobble's Knot), and not to forget Maniac's amazing athletic abilities that inspire "the legend." In short, it is a book written in a flashy, fast-paced style (highlighted by vivid *similes*, colorful adjectives and verbs, *personification*) but also a profound story that exposes many of man's faults, yet promotes the idea that goodness prevails. Maniac finds a home in the end. If he doesn't help the McNabs see the light, perhaps he has helped MarsBar do so.

Maniac is a complex hero who tries desperately to save Russell and Piper McNab from the pathetic trappings of their father's ignorance and intolerance, yet freezes when it comes time to rescue them from the oncoming trolley, leaving it up to MarsBar to save the day. (Note: Maniac's parents were killed when their trolley went off the tracks.) He is heroic yet human, fearless at times, yet haunted and hurt by the loss of his parents. Meanwhile, through the adventures of young Jeffrey Magee the author reminds us of the kindness of strangers, the crippling effects of fear, the importance of education, and that East Enders and West Enders can live, work, and play together.

Maniac Magee is also a great book to use for teaching *personification, simile, symbolism, allusion, irony, alliteration* and *assonance*. Examples of these abound in Mr. Spinelli's slap-happy prose. Mr. Spinelli especially loves *personification* and *simile* and provides excellent examples for teaching these poetic devices. He describes Christmas morning, "Within an hour or two, the holiday would come bounding down the stairs and squealing 'round the tinseled trees of Two Mills. But for the moment, Christmas bided its time outside, a purer presence." (Also note the *alliteration* and *assonance* all at work here.) A few chapters later "January slipped an icy finger under his collar and down his back," and then "During the night, March doubled back and grabbed April by the scruff of the neck and flung it another week or two down the road." Around every corner in Mr. Spinelli's work *similes* jump out at you: "It was a strange voice, deep and thick and sort of clotted, as though it had to fight its way through a can of worms before coming out"; "He ran a hand along the wall. The peeling paint came off like cornflakes"; "They tore into the bag like jackals into carrion"; "When Arnold came to and discovered this, he took off like a horsefly from a swatter." You can discuss *symbolism* and *allusion*. Mr. Spinelli describes an unaccounted-for period of time in Maniac's life as "The Lost Year." He sleeps in the buffalo pen at the zoo (similar to a manger), becomes fascinated with the story of the Children's Crusade, meets the Pickwells, a family of good Samaritans who despite not having much money, but who always have room at their dinner table for people who are down and out. And, of course, Maniac dares to walk into and live in the East End where "For the life of him, he couldn't figure why these East Enders called themselves black. He kept looking and looking, and the colors he found were gingersnap and light fudge and dark fudge and acorn and butter rum and cinnamon and burnt orange. But never licorice, which, to him, was real black."

Maniac Magee provides fuel for much thought and discussion. It touches upon subjects and themes that I am passionate about (baseball, race relations, tolerance of others, fitting in), so each year when we read it, I feel a real commitment to helping the students discover the book's worth and relevance. Teachers need to find such books they feel so strongly about. Feed off the students' energy, but also your own.

Into Hope: Maya Angelou and the Real Life Ballad

On our last full day in Jamaica last year I dragged my wife Vicki into a cab for a harrowing, knuckle-clenching trip down the mountain road that led us to 56 Hope Road in Kingston. I had resolved that no matter what, I was going to visit the Bob Marley Museum, having been so inspired and educated and reminded and comforted by his music ever since I first heard those words, "One good thing about music when it hits you feel no pain." After we arrived and parked, Vicki immediately stumbled out into the sweet scented air and flopped down on the steps while I looked into purchasing tickets for the tour. When I returned I noticed her chatting with a burly Jamaican and an old timer Rasta character who turned out to be Georgie, Bob's friend from Trenchtown mentioned in his song "No Woman No Cry." They told her it was the sudden change in altitude and suggested she chill a spell. I, meanwhile, was discovering a remarkable music that was blasting out across the courtyard. It happened to be three songs performed by Bob's children, Ziggy Marley and the Melody Makers off their CD *Spirit of*

Music. I had not experienced such an immediate connection to new, unknown to me music since I had heard Ani DiFranco's "Cradle and All" back in the early 90's. After listening to the Bob Marley story courtesy of our guide and a twenty-minute movie, Vicki declared that Jamaica would be the perfect place for Montessori (she being a teacher trainer of said educational philosophy). I remarked, "Vick, I've got to find that CD when I get back to the States."

Upon our return home, I went out and found *Spirit of Music.* Meanwhile, a few weeks later, Vicki received messages that Sharon Marley, daughter of Bob and one of the Melody Makers, had learned of Vicki's training program from a friend in Miami and wanted to inquire about enrolling. As they corresponded, Sharon became fascinated with Vicki's proclamation about bringing Montessori to Jamaica and why it came to her at the museum. As it happens Sharon runs a day care center and school in Kingston and was interested in the Montessori method. By the following autumn Vicki was helping her new Jamaican friend convert the school into a Montessori environment. Happy coincidence? Pre-destiny? A simple twist of fate? To me the idea of the daughter of Bob Marley, a fabulous talent and successful performer in her own right, resolving to dedicate much of her time and energy to helping educate the children of Kingston, Jamaica cannot help but make a person smile and feel good about the human race.

Some years back I had a smile on when I heard Maya Angelou's inaugural poem, "On the Pulse of Morning." She spoke with such hard-earned faith about facing our country's painful past and reminding us of our "promises to keep." Within days I was typing a song lyric in tribute to her.

Into Hope

I've heard you know why the caged bird sings,
The sounds of silence sorrow brings,
I heard you broke free upon angel wings
And soared inside of you.

Where do you put what your heart hates to know?
How do you take the pain and make it into hope?
Maya Angelou

Stripped away from your ma and your pa,
Sent down river to Arkansas
Where God couldn't save you from man's law
But that ain't nothin' new.

Then it happened when you were eight.
He got your body but your soul escaped.
You could have grown up one more victim of hate,
But God's love stuck in you.

Where do you put what your heart hates to know?
How do you take the pain and make it into hope?
Maya Angelou

They say the phoenix rose from the ash,
The future is only as close as the past,
Forgiveness is the hardest thing to ask.
You've got a lot inside of you.

You didn't just stop, you decided to go,
Follow the river wherever it'd flow,
Every baby born's got a right to grow,
There's just so much a body can do.

Where do you put what your heart hates to know?
How do you take the pain and make it into hope?
Maya Angelou

I've heard you know why the caged bird sings,
The sounds of silence sorrow brings,
I heard you broke free upon angel wings
And soared inside of you.

Her remarkable story of overcoming a barrage of hardships and not only persevering but inspiring others to do so reminds me of Jackie Robinson. Hers is another excellent example of good character and thus worthy of creating a lesson around. As an English teacher, I consider her reading of "On the Pulse of Morning" at President Clinton's first inauguration an extraordinary reminder of how poetry is part of an oral tradition. The poem itself has plenty of *allusions* and symbolism to discuss, while any number of interviews with Maya Angelou are worth seeking out. In particular, Lawrence Toppman's 1993 piece entitled "Maya Angelou: The Serene Spirit of a Survivor" is a fine source for Ms. Angelou's views on writing and performing. Exposure to poetry of such depth can inspire young people to dig deeper in their own writing. After being introduced to the work of Maya Angelou, a young girl named Ellen wrote a poem she titled "Writing is my blood." In it she captured how writing can be a lifeline (as it was for Ms. Angelou):

As I fall there's no one to help me up,
As I hurt there's no one who cares,
So I look around to see who is left,
And there's a pen and a pad lying there.
And maybe, just maybe, I pick them both up,
And I might even begin to write,
And maybe I start to feel a bit better
In spite of my sadness and fright.
And as my thoughts flow I can begin to tell
Of the world I've only seen in my dreams,
And as I look out and peer through the glass
The world's not as bad as it seems.

This is powerful poetry. "Into Hope", on the other hand, qualifies not as standard poetry but is a *ballad* which is a very old form of song poetry. The earliest poems and songs told stories and reading and writing and singing ballads can be another cross-pollination project, this time with the music department or a faculty member who plays a musical instrument. I usually introduce my lesson on ballads with "The Ballad of Gilligan's Isle" which is familiar, easy and fun to memorize and sing as a class. A much older one worth preserving is "The Fox" who goes out on a chilly night to rob the farmer's hen house so he and his family can feast. This is a terrific piece to use when discussing *narrative point of view*.

Point of view. It's always critical to consider when groping towards understanding. Miss Gibb years ago introduced me to a profound modern day *parable*, author unknown, entitled "The Little Boy."

Once a little boy went to school.
He was quite a little boy
And it was quite a big school.
But when the little boy
Found that he could get to his room
By walking right in from the door outside,
The school did not seem
Quite so big any more.

One morning
When the little boy had been in school awhile
The teacher said,
"Today we are going to make a picture."
"Good," thought the little boy.
He liked to make pictures.
He could make all kinds:
Lions and tigers, chickens and cows,
Trains and boats.
And he took out his box of crayons
And began to draw.

But the teacher said, "Wait.
It is not time to begin."
And she waited until everyone looked ready.

"Now," said the teacher,
"We are going to make flowers."
"Good," thought the little boy.
He liked to make flowers,
And he began to make beautiful ones
With his pink and orange and blue crayons.

But the teacher said, "wait,
And I will show you how."
And she drew a flower on the blackboard.
It was red with a green stem.
"There," said the teacher,

"Now you may begin."

The little boy looked at the teacher's flower.
Then he looked at his own flower.
He liked his flower better than the teacher's,
But he did not say this.
He just turned his paper over
And made a flower like the teacher's.
It was red with a green stem.

On another day
When the little boy had opened
The door from the outside all by himself,
The teacher said,
"Today we are going to make something with clay."
"Good!" thought the little boy.
He liked clay.
He could make all kinds of things with clay:
Elephants and mice,
Cars and trucks,
And he began to pull and pinch
His ball of clay.

But the teacher said,
"Wait. It is not time to begin."
And she waited until everyone looked ready.

"Now," said the teacher,
"We are going to make a dish."
"Good!" thought the little boy.
He liked to make dishes.
And he began to make some
That were all shapes and sizes.

But the teacher said, "Wait,
And I will show you how."
And she showed everyone how to make
One deep dish.

"There," said the teacher,
"Now you may begin."

The little boy looked at the teacher's dish.
Then he looked at his own.
He liked his dishes better than the teacher's,
But he did not say this.
He just rolled the clay into a big ball again
And made a dish like the teacher's.
It was a deep dish.

And pretty soon
The little boy learned to wait
And to watch
And to make things just like the teacher.
And pretty soon
He didn't make things of his own any more.

Then it happened
That the little boy and his family
Moved to another city,
And the little boy
Had to go to another school.

This school was even bigger
Than the other one,
And there was no door from the outside
Into his room.
He had to go up more big steps
And walk down a long hall
To get to his room.

And the very first day
He was there
The teacher said,
"Today we are going to make a picture."

"Good!" thought the little boy,
and he waited for the teacher
to tell him what to do.
But the teacher didn't say anything.
She just walked around the room.

When she came to the little boy
She said, "Don't you want to make a picture?"
"Yes," said the little boy.
"What are you going to make?"
"I don't know until you make it," said the little boy.
"How shall I make it?"
"Why any way you like," said the teacher.
"And any color?" asked the little boy.
"Any color," said the teacher.
"If everyone makes the same picture
and uses the same colors
how would I know who made what
and which was which?"

"I don't know," said the little boy.
And he began to draw a flower.
It was red with a green stem.

This piece struck a chord with me that shall reverberate as long as I ply my craft. Beware of cookie cutter teaching methods. Require standards and insist on students learning formats and patterns, even formulas where appropriate, but do not strip them of their creative selves. Allow young people the opportunity to express themselves in their own ways, praise each piece's potential as well as good points and only then carefully critique areas in need of revision or alterations. That's my mantra.

5

Thoughts on Kids and Writing

An Answer is Born

I had heard the question many times before. Especially since I allow for student input involving the shaping of writing assignments, there are always those students who need the comfort of specific guidelines and set boundaries. There are also boys and girls who would happily prefer not to expend too much time and energy into another writing assignment, and so the question is ever-present, lurking in the minds of the anxious and uninspired. For years I handled it with my own uncertain brand of caution and care. I would give them a minimum number of words and offer that the truly adventuresome were not restricted to any set in stone number. If I had a student who trembled at the thought of writing a full page, I would write the first couple sentences and ask him to now add on to what I had written, while conversely I would accept fifteen-page stories and go over the piece, making editing suggestions to the student. I have always tried to adapt and adjust to each individual student's needs as a young writer.

Then one day a seventh grader named Matt asked me the question again. "Mr. Winans, how long does it have to be?" Off the cuff I replied, "As long as it interests me." This made Matt smirk and reply, "No, seriously, Mr. Winans, how many pages do I have to write?" I repeated myself, savoring the sound and priding myself on coming up with a keeper for future encounters with the dreaded question. Ah, as long as it interests me. The kind of reply that perhaps might make a student think about it. An open-ended reply that does not confine the young writer nor does it let him off easily. Other teachers certainly must have used this line before me, but I was excited because when I happened to come upon it I felt I had earned the right to use that phrase. Length by itself never impressed me. Saying something simple in a unique or fresh way, trying out new vocabulary words even if awkwardly at first, writing something heartfelt, writing something that excited the student enough to want to share it with others…this is the writing I look for and cherish every year. The length of an assignment is often foremost on the minds of some students, and there are many school writing assignments where length is a factor and consideration. But making length a destination to get to, a marker of completion, a burden to bear is neither necessary nor sensible for many creative or expository writing assignments.

In this day and age of the computer, I have noticed that students do write longer, more developed compositions. The use of computers and laptop programs has helped make many students (especially those with poor hand-eye skills) feel more comfortable about writing longer compositions; yet these longer pieces must be scrutinized and you, the teacher, must then show the student how to edit the work and not merely depend on spell check or grammar check. By seventh grade, I talk to the students about saying more with less. I introduce the word "pithy" and on occasion have given them just a little taste of Shakespeare's *Romeo and Juliet*, though I do not linger in the great Bard's world for long because sometimes "a man's got to know his limitations" and, therefore, for their sake I tell my students that Shakespeare is for later. Plays, however, tell involved, lengthy stories in a time-conscious and space-confined venue. In fact, one-act plays, short stories, and poetry all require a certain amount of precision with words and making statements in a more concise manner. As long as the thought is complete or the detail enough to create a clear picture, being economical is a good thing. But in suggesting this idea you must also emphasize the need to be choosy when selecting words. Instead of writing, "It had rained the night before. So the ground was wet. I saw the cat running around the backyard. Leaves were flying everywhere. On the street, a dog caught scent of the mad cat and bounded towards it," you could write, "In our backyard I watched the fitful cat scatter soggy leaves as nearby an alerted dog approached." This skill is not difficult to practice. Make up some paragraphs of five to six sentences, each describing a scene. Then ask the students to rewrite the paragraphs using two to three sentences that must include all of the information, but in fewer words. As with anything else, saying more with less takes practice (ah, an off-rhyme).

Allowing Ellen to be Ellen

Erica Jong once confessed, "I went for years not finishing anything. Because, of course, when you finish something you can be judged." This fear grips many of us, and students who may not be self-conscious in fifth grade are by their seventh grade year and thus less inclined to be themselves in their writing and less willing to share their work with the rest of the class. How does one counter this impediment to establishing the right environment for open communication? Being open-minded enough to allow students some say in what they write about and how they write it has worked for me. You still must challenge them with demands of the craft (including correct spelling and mechanics on final drafts), but allow yourself to listen to their alternative ideas for story lines and not be so quick to impose your own adult perceptions on their requests to write nonsense or horror or stories based on video games. You can scoff at these topics as irrelevant or just a byproduct of an adolescent phase, but they are important to the students and therefore valid material for writing. Above all, mix the serious with the silly. We tend to push young people too quickly towards the rigors, requirements and routines of adulthood, and that's pure robbery in my humble view. After taking tests, students need to run off steam, play Seven-Up or Trivial Pursuit, have the opportunity to tell silly jokes in class.

Teachers, meanwhile, need to be mindful that our job not only demands that we instruct, listen, and advise, but also expose children to ideas without imposing our own views (be they religious, political, psychological, philosophical). Teachers need to be aware that having opinions and passing judgment are two separate things. Instead of dismissing rap music or paint-balling or shows such as "South Park," the adult who does not rush to judgment but instead allows young people their passions and talks to them about these interests will more likely gain their respect. You can give your opinion and even be critical of songs that use profanity or shows that sink to toilet humor, but do not be so hasty and dismissive of their value (even if purely as entertainment no more no less). Just as we dare not underestimate what young people are capable of accomplishing in the various academic areas, we cannot undervalue who they are, which they in part associate with these extracurricular activities. This may sound contradictory to what I espoused earlier about the perils of this age of too much time spent in front of computer games and game boys and television screens, but I am comfortable with the contradiction. I am critical sometimes, but I try to be mindful of who I was and how I felt when I was the age of my students, and it usually brings me down to earth or at least to a better level of understanding.

I know of what I speak. You gain students' respect through respecting them. Some years back a girl named Ellen, one of my most promising student writers because she was unafraid, kept me on my toes, often suggesting the class activity or writing assignment needed spicing up, and because of her and her very talented classmates I kept revising, even completely redesigning ideas for writing assignments for them. I was invigorated because these students were willing and eager to write as long as I made the assignment interesting enough. After teaching this group of youngsters, I realized this was my destiny; whether it disappointed others or not, I was meant to remain working with and hopefully inspiring fifth and seventh graders to become more confident, willing young writers. As for Ellen, she unleashed ideas and painted dreamscapes in words and wrote as if she were searching for the meaning of life. Her effort and willingness to be open were inspirational, and I believe, in part, possible because she was allowed to be herself, and I encouraged it with occasional suggestions, but never criticisms. In her thank you note to me at graduation, Ellen mentioned how much my support meant to her and she thanked me for patience, laughing with the students, and even "all those times you made us do awful things like grammar. I feel queasy at the mere thought. I can't believe I'm thanking you for grammar." Then Ellen wrote so succinctly and profoundly, "Thanks for understanding that we're kids and yet not treating us like we are." Excuse me if it sounds as if I'm beating my own drum or blowing my own horn here, but that line floored me. Over the years others had alluded to the reason students seemed to appreciate their time spent with me, but no one had said it quite so well, so poetically, if you will. It was and remains the greatest compliment I have ever received.

It's a tough standard for any teacher to keep up with, and I don't always do it. But if I can offer any sage advice to young teachers I would direct them to this: Understand where your students are coming from and what their needs are, and then try to blend your own with theirs. Be firm with standards and grammar and curriculum requirements, but also be flexible to suggestions and requests from your students. Allow that they can guide you as well as you them.

The Constant Quest: Avoiding Complacency

I'm often at a loss when it comes to outlining my fifth and seventh grade school year curriculum agenda at our annual beginning of the year parents' night because I honestly do not always know in which direction we will be headed at that point. I certainly know what grammar and mechanics we must cover and some of the books we will be reading, but so much is subject to change depending upon where the students' interests lie. A few years back the fifth graders loved to draw and we spent extra time in class showing the students who were less confident how to add illustrations to their stories. The following year the fives spent every homeroom singing and dancing so we devoted two months to putting together a talent show without sacrificing the other academic work. Some of the more rebellious or resistant students became much more cooperative in the classroom once I gave them the opportunity to express themselves through performance art.

It has been suggested that teaching gets easier the longer you do it. I think it's true that you learn about pacing and gain more mastery of your subject and therefore more confidence. But there is also the danger of becoming too comfortable and complacent. As much as I speak here of following where the students lead me, I also spend equal amounts of time leading them when I instruct them in lessons on vocabulary building, grammar and mechanics, and reading comprehension. There are days when I feel flat and that I failed to connect with the students. One of my weaknesses as a teacher (and I have plenty) is becoming easily bored with what I consider the more mundane but equally important elements of language—parts of speech, spelling rules, and other utilitarian aspects necessary to know in order to be effective writers.

Some days I even bore myself during these lessons. Capitalization and punctuation rules need to be taught, but I catch that look in my students' eyes which is like looking into a mirror that reflects back an image of myself at their age. Some things that have to be done are just no fun so that's why I like Miss Gibb's idea of lollipops at grammar time. "A spoonful of sugar makes the medicine go down."

One obvious way to avoid complacency as a creative writing teacher is to be on the lookout for new writing ideas. Recent events from the newspaper, current fads or popular genres, or games the students appear to be excited about can be a springboard for story ideas. Another trick I use is revising earlier writing assignments, updating them if you will. I once devised an assignment entitled "My Own Museum." I wanted the students to understand *symbol* and use *detail* from their own lives. I asked them to "write a composition (roughly two pages typed) in which you describe objects, artifacts, or personal possessions that you would have on display if you owned a museum. The objects can be viewed as symbols which represent your interests, dreams, goals, hobbies, beliefs and/or personal preferences. You can also describe what your museum would look like, where you would locate it, and when visiting hours would be. Be serious about this assignment, but remember what the ice cream man said: 'Humor is good.' You must describe a minimum of seven objects in your museum. You can name your museum if you like and explain why you've chosen a particular building design and location. Be thoughtful and creative. Write with intense purpose." A few years later I recast the assignment as "My Own Tree House" in which they had to include personal possessions and other objects that represent what is important to them. This class was, as a whole, more outdoorsy and many were more likely to have spent considerable time up a tree. One young girl wrote about having an opening in the roof so she could watch the stars at night which would help her to dream. One of the boys described a multi-leveled complex (complete with pool and arcade room) which obviously would require a grove of redwoods to support its size and weight. From the practical to the fantastical, students always provide a wonderful variety of visions on such assignments. Reading their individual descriptions of museums and tree houses or other imagined worlds helps make the task of teaching grammar far more tolerable. It's my sugar.

"Don't Be Afraid to Fail"

In Ken Burns' monumental eighteen-hour history of baseball, the narrative thread is masterfully voiced by long-time nightly news anchor John Chancellor and an eclectic, well-informed and sincerely impassioned group of expert fans including historian Shelby Foote, political commentator George Will, baseball writer Roger Angel, ex-ballplayers Bill Lee and Buck O'Neill, and the historian Doris Kearns who has experienced life both as a Brooklyn Dodgers rooter and a Boston Red Sox devotee. Her thoughts on the 1967 "Impossible Dream" season of the Red Sox lead her to describe Carl Yastremski's Triple Crown year and she marvels at how he seemed to want to be at the plate when everything was on the line. Kearns notes that most of us might cower at having to assume such a role, but that Yaz thrived on the challenge and came through almost every time "or so it seemed." Earlier in the series, Burns' narrator points out that failure itself is well understood in the game of baseball for even its greatest practitioners of hitting fail seven out of ten times at the plate. I like to utilize this observation when discussing creative writing with young people. I tell them, "Don't be afraid to fail. Take chances by using new words, phrasing ideas differently, saying things you're not sure of, exploring where ideas might take you." Some years back, the mother of one of my former students approached me at a social function in our new gymnasium. She had an uneven smirk and a story with an ending she wasn't giving away to tell. Apparently her daughter, when applying to one of the Ivy League schools, determined not to complete the application form with the standard essay but instead chose to create a response with a collage of words and pictures. Her mother reiterated to me how she was quite concerned that the admissions people might not react positively to such an offbeat approach, and her daughter replied something to the effect that it was okay because Mr. Winans always told her to take risks and be brave as a writer. Now if I didn't know at that time that her daughter was already at Princeton I might have been looking for the nearest avenue of escape, but it was obvious that she was thanking me for helping encourage such confidence (or recklessness) in her daughter. All I could tell her was that it sounded like something I might have said, all the while thinking to myself, "These kids really do listen and occasionally even pick up on my little rants." Good thing she was skilled enough to get away with such brazen individuality.

But isn't that the point? If we commit to the idea of promoting creative writing, don't we also assume the responsibility of encouraging young people to "think outside the box" as current educational "experts" call it? As an aside here (one of those deviations) this au currant phrase amuses me. How are we supposed to hope for young people thinking outside a box when we sleep on a box in a walled-in box within a big box where we put our food in an ice box and eat cereal out of a box and then head off to go to school or work in boxes within bigger boxes only to return to sit in front of the boob box? Melissa Gilbert's hero in *The Last American Man* recently spoke of this, as did folksinger Pete Seeger fifty years ago in "Little Boxes." I can relate to these voices crying out in the wilderness. I can also agree that colleges and the world at large need creative thinkers who can think outside the box. Given the opportunity, I've seen young people do this all the time in homeroom moments doodling on the black board, in free associating conversations at recess, during those in-between moments at play rehearsals. Don't quiet them down at these times but suggest they channel what they're saying or doing into something concrete, a work of art. Seize on these moments, these glimpses of free thought and undiluted expression.

Because of Hugh

He was without doubt the weirdest looking college professor I ever had. Not at all what I had imagined going in. Sandals, flared cords, a bead necklace, scraggly hair and goatee, waving a Tipperillo, his eyes bursting with light and mischief (my students Jason and Ellen had the same eyes). He never seemed to know exactly what was going to happen and he always asked us what was on our good minds. He spoke in waves and pauses and sudden bursts of fantastic thought, and he never failed to listen as intensely as he spoke, and I knew immediately without thinking about it or being able to explain the reasoning behind my decision that here was my college mentor. He was really pleased that I was familiar with Wordsworth's Tinturn Abbey, and I was knocked out by Brian Patten's *Notes to the Hurrying Man* which Hugh gave us as an initiation text. Later, he would put me through my paces writing my thesis on John Keats and it was he who insisted I take classes with older, experienced English majors and that, despite my shyness, I contribute to class discussions. He placed faith in me and insisted I live up to his faith.

When it came to writing, Hugh Ogden didn't teach me so much how to write; more importantly, he taught me why to write, and for that I am forever in his debt. These feelings we feel, these questions we have about who we are and why we are and how we got to be where we are, these crazy thoughts that don't immediately make sense or seem to fit in with what we've been programmed to understand, count as much as any other man's and are worth exploring and finding out more about. We write in search of meaning and perhaps hopefully enlightenment. We write to understand better ourselves and the world around us. Keats was Cortez on that rock. Hugh taught me that.

There were others. At Brooks School, Reverend George Voight insisted I be confirmed and then dragged me to nursing homes and after school centers advising me that it was our duty to give to others. Also at Brooks, Jake Dunnell introduced me to introspection and the juxtaposition of man's folly and potential. Once when I was worried about where I would end up at college, Jake reassured me that I would make the most of wherever I went, and I'll never forget standing in his dimly lit study feeling emboldened and a little better prepared for the unknown. It is that simple encouragement and faith in young people that I gained from these people and hope to impart in my students.

Twelve Thoughts

As I continue on this adventure otherwise known as teaching or my chosen vocation, I occasionally have the good fortune to discover like-minded advocates of children who, in my humble opinion, make sense. One such individual is Dr. Mel Levine who has spent a good part of his lifetime studying and working with young people to solve the gigantic puzzle of how different kids learn differently in order to empower students and teachers alike to solve learning problems. He is a mild-mannered man with an amazing mind and an affinity for geese. His talk to a group of teachers from various schools in south Florida one day in January of 2001 deeply resonated with me. I remember taking reams of notes and later read many of his quotes to my seventh graders. The general consensus amongst my students was that Dr. Levine understood young people, and they wished he was their teacher. I concurred wholeheartedly. Following are twelve thoughts from that talk.

"You can remember something without having understood it and you can understand something without remembering it."

"There should be no labeling. Let's be D-free and reserve judgment."

"Nothing requires more energy than sitting in a chair."

"Schools should teach children how to learn; parents should teach children how to work."

"Shouldn't we be developing reflective minds, not impulsive minds? In other words, shouldn't we teach kids to think slowly? Therefore, what about untimed tests?"

"Time management should be part of every course a student takes."

"How important are memory skills? Rote regurgitation is useless later in life. Are we preparing students to be master regurgitators or good at understanding?"

"School is one big social trial. The goal for most kids each day is to avoid humiliation."

"Kids don't always know how what they say or how they say it comes across."

"A kid who cannot remember school subject matter can speak eloquently of and remember everything about baseball…that is, domain specific…so can you tailor learning to include more assignments around this domain?"

"What about kids who have too much success too early on? Isn't that a bubble that's going to burst? Everyone has to deal with feelings of inadequacy…isn't it better if it happened a bit earlier on, not suddenly later in life?"

"Adults who do well quite often as kids were kids who had passions."

I hope Dr. Levine will excuse some paraphrasing in one or two places where my notes were scribbled. Much of what he says here goes against the grain of contemporary (or archaic) educational thought. Yet, I deeply believe he is speaking truth and pointing us in the direction we need to be headed. I try to apply his idea of tailoring "domain specific" writing assignments around students' interests. We talk about and sometimes write about the social element and how young people similar to adults can hurt one another without even knowing it. And ultimately, if we are successful the students and I tap into, explore and exploit their passions just as I introduce mine (baseball, poetry, music, history) to them. At some point in high school and later in college in the classrooms of a half dozen teachers learning became a magical journey to me, an awakening and a discovery, a place where hope itself still exists. Hope is an essential comfort to a Red Sox fan, a loyal companion to a hopeless romantic, and a tonic for what ails these cynical times.

Left to Write

What is there left to write? I want to throw a few random thoughts and quotes your way before putting this baby to bed. Roland Barth has said that schools must offer "low anxiety and high standards." Steve Clem once told a group of us teachers that "it's always better for a student to create an answer than choose an answer." An ex-classmate of mine and fellow educator Bill Engel points out in *Education and Anarchy* that "teachers remain learners themselves even (and especially) when teaching" and "education is about letting learning happen." All of these sentiments and exhortations ring true in my mind, and I am greatly comforted to know such people are out there spreading the word through lectures and articles and books. Meanwhile, each summer by the beginning of August, I begin again anxiously pondering a new school year. Where will it lead us this time? What will I try differently and what do these new youngsters have in mind? I think of the final stanza of Seamus Heaney's poem "At the Wellhead" about a neighborhood girl Rosie Keenan who is blind:

She knew us by our voices. She'd say she "saw"
Whoever or whatever. Being with her
Was intimate and helpful, like a cure
You didn't notice happening. When I read
A poem with Keenan's well in it, she said,
"I can see the sky at the bottom of it now."

I want my students to discover the sky at the bottom of the well. Being with them is my cure which I have grown keenly aware of and ever more appreciative of.

Recently a seventh grader wrote in her journal what was on her good mind that day.

In the beginning there was time and there was space, and now just like our ozone layer, both are deteriorating. But what does this mean? Does it mean that the world is running out of time and will soon meet its doom? Or does it mean that the walls of the universe are closing in on us so there is less and less room? The first statement means none of these things. It simply means that we have made our own lives too stressful, too complicated and too busy. Our streets are too crowded, our minds are too full. We have no time to spend with our families because all our spare time is spent at school and work. But what do we work for? At school we learn to get jobs. At our jobs we work to earn money for the families we never even see. We have created too much stress for ourselves and this is because of money and greed. Why is it so important that we learn how to identify a gerund, the anatomy of a starfish and who the king of England was in 1603? If teachers spend all day with kids, then why do some of them seem to hate us? We've brought too many things upon ourselves that have done us no good, things like stress and disease. If there's controversy, why not let it go instead of starting a war, killing hundreds and losing anyway? Some people ignore this topic. Others acknowledge it but still don't want to do anything about it, but maybe there is no solution. Maybe there is no solution, and since teachers seem to have all the answers, tell me teacher, what do we do now?

The student actually shared this with another teacher who had cheerfully asked what she was writing so intensely in study hall one afternoon. A few days later at lunch, my colleague and I were discussing examples of recent student writing and she mentioned the piece to me, so I asked the girl if I might read the journal entry, and she somewhat reluctantly gave it to me because she felt it wasn't really good writing, just some thoughts she had scribbled down after finishing her other work. The main theme was one she and others had wrestled with in recent years, the seeming overload of activity and "busy-ness" that gobbles up our days. Working parents and conscientious seventh graders both feel this pressure and mourn the lack of quiet, down time. Meanwhile, students have to deal with seven or eight different teachers in their daily lives and stressed teachers can "seem to hate" kids in the eyes of students. The young writer was right. The writing itself was marginal compared to her work for me on other assignments, but there was a provocative nature to the piece that led me to respond in kind.

"What do we do now? We do what we can. Little things. Simple gestures. Say something nice to your brother like wishing him good luck on a quiz day. Enjoy the change in weather that signals holidays are around the bend. Have faith in your teachers even when you don't understand the significance of the assignments, but also know they are as human as you are and get frustrated and angry and yes, stressed just like anybody else, and Lord knows we make mistakes. Don't think there are not nights when teachers toss and turn all night because of situations with students that they haven't gotten a handle on yet. You're right, the 'world is too much with us' as the poet Wordsworth once wrote. Modern life is on spin cycle and not healthy unless we figure out how to find balance. Life is a journey in which each of us seeks our own destiny which isn't always clear to us. We grope in the dark, longing for order when sometimes there's only chaos. Sometimes we laugh and crack jokes to mask our insecurities and fears. Young people in their early teens are in a tough position. They begin to see more clearly the world's hypocrisy and it confuses them. They naturally question authority and want freedom from its restraints, yet some flounder when coming to grips with the responsibility that goes hand in hand with freedom. Television tells you image is everything, bigger is better, more is not enough. You're told to get good grades, not to learn something new every day. 'Money doesn't talk it swears, obscenity who really cares? Propaganda all is phony.' Remember those lines from the song I read to you? Greed is a problem. Daily life does seem like a vicious cycle that leaves us overwhelmed. Young people have long spoken out about this crazy, mixed-up world, and in speaking out, you are using language to communicate and in so doing seek dialogue which presents questions and sometimes allows us to arrive at answers. Not always, mind you. Sometimes questions can only find answers after a long search, and subjects such as history and science make greater sense when all that you've learned is one day put together to reveal to you how complicated and yet interconnected the world is. The Indians studied nature to teach them how to live, and we can learn much from the wind and starfish just as we can better understand and appreciate (and fight for if we have to) our constitutional rights and protected freedoms of religion and speech, so knowing about King George and why the Colonists eventually went to war against England is important even if it seems dry and irrelevant at the moment. (By the way who was the King of England in 1603?) Young people can be impatient, and life takes more time than we're sometimes willing to give it. Yet young people also have a great advantage over many adults. You believe things can get better, that 'hope springs eternal.' So what to do? Go on believing and 'keep busy being born instead of dying.' Question authority politely. Go on asking questions and speaking your mind. Remember that when 'everyone thinks alike nobody thinks.' And most of all, some advice my dad gave me that he got from his boarding school headmaster, 'Accept a person for who he is and then try to find the good in him.' I think you are well-equipped to understand and appreciate that bit of advice, and, of course, write on."

Postscript: Moondog Matinee

Maybe subconsciously the title ***Moondog Verse*** came to me from memories of Sunday nights at boarding school back in the early 70's listening to Wolfman Jack's oldies radio show which was as close as I got to experiencing Alan Freed's Moondog Matinee broadcasts unleash rock 'n roll on the unsuspecting world. I felt that first flush of discovering something magical listening to Bill Haley's Comets and Junior Walker's All-Stars wailing saxophones and Chuck Berry's prescient poetry in "Nadine," lines such as "I saw her walking by a coffee colored Cadillac" and "Oh Nadine, honey is that you? Seems like every time I catch up to you you've got something else to do." The sounds and word imagery from the early days of this new musical form comforted my adolescent heartbreak but also resonated innocence and hopefulness; such a contrast to what was going on at the time in contemporary radio. Students in elementary and middle school are still at or close enough to that age of hopefulness that I found in such music. They are equipped with energy, earnestness, an eagerness to please, a willingness to explore their imaginations and break from conventional formats, so they are essentially primed to try anything. Writing teachers of this age group have a golden opportunity to get kids hooked on writing. Writing days in my classroom are my Moondog Matinee.

So here we are at the end of July, the dog days of summer having arrived. A new school year appears just over the horizon. A teacher's life is constantly new beginnings, perhaps one of its greatest rewards. Writing this was a cool morning breeze, and I hope it offers you a few ideas, maybe an alternative approach to coaxing some good writing out of your students. Just remember to guide but also more importantly follow, listen as thoughtfully as you speak, show them your world but acknowledge and get to know theirs, always seek and refuse to stagnate, and keep coming up with writing ideas from your own and your students' interests. There's much great verse yet to be written. Let's work to bring it out.

Glossary of Terms

Alliteration is the technique of linking words together by repeating the same sound at the beginning of two or more words next to or near each other.
Which way does the wind blow?

Allusion is a reference to a usually well-known person, place or thing not directly stated, but hinted at.
He felt like a defeated general, his stringy blond hair soon to be some warrior's war trophy alludes to General Custer and his defeat at the Little Big Horn.

Assonance is the use of repetition in vowel sounds in words close to one another.
The old oak grows slowly but steadily.

Ballad can be a narrative poem or a type of folk song which tells a story, often with a moral to it.

Characters are the personalities in a story. They can be people, animals or fantasy creatures. The most important character is the **main character**, while other characters are called **secondary** or **supporting** characters. The good character or hero of the story is referred to as the **protagonist**. His or her adversary or the villain is called the **antagonist**. Often, the main character has a **character flaw** which is a weakness that puts the character in danger.

Climax is the high point or moment of revelation in a story.

Conflict takes many different forms in a story. It can be a problem to be solved, an argument, a battle, inner turmoil experienced by the main character, a predicament or any situation that causes tension. There are four main types of conflict in literature: man verses man, man verses nature, man verses society, and man verses himself.

Creative Writing, in this context, refers to **literary writing** (poetry, lyrics, fiction, and plays) as opposed to other forms of writing taught in school, i.e. expository, descriptive and assertive writing(essays, thesis, editorial, article, report).

However, as noted in the text, all writing requires creativity and good creative writing is often expository, descriptive and assertive.

Dialect is a style of writing that attempts to capture the way ordinary people speak in a specific region or time period. There are many different dialects presented in Mark Twain's *The Adventures of Huckleberry Finn*.
"Dat dere truck is trash, Huck."

Dialogue is conversation that takes place between two or more characters in a story. It normally appears in quotation marks. A **monologue** is a lengthy, uninterrupted speech by one character, while a **soliloquy** is a monologue spoken in a play.

Dictation is an exercise in which the teacher reads aloud one line at a time a poem or passage that the students, in turn, carefully listen to and then write down on a piece of paper.

Free verse is poetry written without specific meter or regular rhyme pattern. Instead it establishes rhythm through **typography**, repetition and other sound devices such as **assonance** and **alliteration,** though this is not required.

Genre refers to the three types of literary writing (fiction, poetry and drama). **Sub-genres** are specific types of fiction writing that share common elements and characteristics. Examples include science fiction, mystery and suspense, and westerns.

Hyperbole is deliberate, often extreme exaggeration used as a figure of speech.
"He was eating a pickle the size of three pregnant watermelons."

Imagery consists of words that help form a picture in the reader's mind. These word pictures evoke one of or a combination of the five senses and help make certain ideas or points of view easier to understand, more interesting or revelatory. Such techniques as **metaphor, simile** and **allusion** are used by poets to create imagery. In "Fern Hill" Dylan Thomas writes:
"All the sun long it was running, it was lovely, the hay
Fields high as the house, the tunes from the chimneys, it was air
And playing, lovely and watery
And the fire green as grass."

Irony is a contrast between what is expected or intended and what actually happens. In *Huckleberry Finn,* Huck wrestles with and then finally determines to help the runaway slave Jim escape to freedom on their raft while, unknowingly having missed the turn in the river, they drift further and further into slave territory. That is **ironic.** Verbal irony, meanwhile, is when a writer deliberately says something that is the opposite of what he means.

Metaphor is an implied comparison of two different things used to suggest or make a point. Maya Angelou, for instance, conveys the idea of words used as weapons in her inaugural poem: *"Your mouths spilling words armed for slaughter."*

Off-rhyme is the use of words close but not identical in sound. A true rhyme would be *best* and *quest,* while an off-rhyme would be *best* and *success.*

Onomatopoeia is words that imitate or sound similar to the object or action being described. Some examples are *buzz, bang, smash* and *rip.*

Parable is a short fictitious story with a moral or religious lesson. **Fables** also are stories with intended truths or lessons. They, however, often involve supernatural happenings or animals speaking and acting like humans.

Personification is the technique of giving things non-human or inanimate the personality traits and actions of humans. Feelings can also be **personified.**
    "A river sings a beautiful song."

Plot is the sequence of events in a short story, novel or play.

Poetry is, according to *Webster's Seventh New Collegiate Dictionary,* "writing that formulates a concentrated imaginative awareness of experience in language chosen and arranged to create a specific emotional response through meaning, sound and rhythm." **Poetry** is compressed language with an emphasis on length of line, sound and rhythm. **Verse** can be synonymous with **poetry** or a less intense form of it.

Point of view refers to the agent through whose eyes and voice the story is told. This is usually done through a character in the story (**first-person narrative**) or by the author or an outside voice (**third-person narrative**).

Prose is any form of writing that uses ordinary speech with lines that are continuous.

Rhyme is the repetition of identical sounds. *Green bean moon loon*

Rhythm is an ordered recurring pattern of stressed and unstressed syllables that establishes a flow of sound. It can be established through repetition, typography, use of meter and type of stanza.

Setting is the time and place in which a story, poem or play takes place.

Simile is an implied comparison of two different things used to make a point, but unlike a **metaphor,** a **simile** is introduced by the words *like* or *as*. *"And fire green as grass"* and *"Though I sang in my chains like the sea"* are two similes from "Fern Hill".

Song lyric is verse written to be accompanied by music. It often employs many of the devices of poetry but is meant to be experienced and can only be truly appreciated as part of a musical context.

Stanza is a set group of lines in a poem. Often poems consist of a series of stanzas. In a song lyric, these are called verses.

Stream of consciousness is a form of writing which reveals an unfiltered, (sometimes even unedited) series of thoughts, feelings and free associations, the goal being self-exploration.

Symbol is an object, action, individual or other which has a range of meaning beyond itself. There are obvious symbols such as *the cross* or *the flag*, but poets often use more subtle symbols such as color or ordinary objects that take on a greater meaning within the context of that particular piece of writing.

Theme is the main idea, primary statement or central concern of a story, play or poem. It is not to be confused with the **message** or **moral** of the story which is a lesson or revealed truth.

Tone is the feeling or emotional element in a piece of writing that usually reflects the author's attitude toward what and whom he is writing about. The use of **tone** helps the writer create a **mood** such as exciting, depressing, eerie or dramatic.

Typography is the arrangement of words, phrases and lines in a poem to create a rhythmical effect.

0-595-33814-3

Printed in the United States
24785LVS00002B/292